Pictorial Orbital Theory

Pictorial Orbital Theory

John M Tedder

Purdie Professor of Chemistry
University of St Andrews

Antony Nechvatal

Senior Lecturer in Chemistry
University of Dundee

Pitman

PITMAN PUBLISHING INC.
1020 Plain Street, Marshfield, Massachusetts 02050

PITMAN PUBLISHING LIMITED
128 Long Acre, London WC2E 9AN

Associated Companies

Pitman Publishing Pty Ltd, Melbourne
Pitman Publishing New Zealand Ltd, Wellington
Copp Clark Pitman, Toronto

© John M Tedder and Antony Nechvatal 1985

First published in Great Britain 1985

Library of Congress Cataloging in Publication Data

Tedder, John M. (John Michael)
  Pictorial Orbital Theory.
  Includes index.
  1. Molecular orbitals.   I. Nechvatal, Antony.
II. Title.
QD461.T34   1985   541.2′2   84-26592
ISBN 0-273-02265-2
ISBN 0-273-01902-3 (PBK.)

British Library Cataloguing in Publication Data

Tedder, John M.
  Pictorial orbital theory.
  1. Molecular orbitals 2. Organic compounds
  I. Title   II. Nechvatal, Antony
  547.1′28   QD461
  ISBN 0-273-02265-2
  ISBN 0-273-01902-3 Pbk

Typeset at The Universities Press (Belfast) Ltd.

Manufactured in Great Britain

Contents

Acknowledgments

The orbital contour pictures are based on those from W. J. Jorgensen and L. Salem *The Organic Chemist's Book of Orbitals*, Academic Press, New York, 1973. There are several more recent calculations available but for pictorial orbital theory Jorgensen and Salem's are more than adequate.

Introduction

Our understanding of organic chemistry has depended on the use of models of increasing complexity. The representation of atoms as hard spheres joined together by sticks has been and remains an important part of the organic chemist's stock in trade. In order to understand the mechanism of many reactions, however, a more sophisticated picture was required and this was provided by Lewis Theory which was developed so successfully by the British chemists Sir Robert Robinson and C. K. Ingold. The use of curved arrows to depict electron migration during a chemical reaction led to a much better understanding of the factors which control chemical reactions. The development of resonance theory by the American Linus C. Pauling and others provided the necessary rationale to an all-embracing pictorial theory. The use of 'canonical forms' or 'resonance hybrids', together with the extensive use of curved arrows, has provided the intellectual background to much of modern organic theory. It is somewhat of a paradox that R. B. Woodward, a supreme master of 'arrow pushing', should have been a prime mover in the development of pictorial orbital theory. A number of reactions (particularly cyclic additions like the Diels–Alder reaction) did not fit very well into the curved arrow or canonical forms concept. Indeed these reactions were sometimes called 'no mechanism reactions'. Woodward and Hoffmann showed that by examining the interaction of the frontier molecular orbitals (i.e. the Highest Occupied and the Lowest Unoccupied orbitals) both the regio- and the stereospecificity could be accounted for. Woodward and Hoffmann's treatment was very quickly assimilated into general organic theory for reactions with a cyclic transition state. At present most books continue to use the 'electronic theory' supplemented by 'resonance theory' to describe the major part of organic chemistry and then develop a pictorial orbital theory especially for cyclic reactions. The purpose of this little book is to show that it is possible to use pictorial orbital theory to describe all the major transformations in organic chemistry. There is no suggestion that a stage has been reached when the 'arrow pushing' of the electronic theory can be completely displaced by the 'balloons and sausages' of pictorial orbital theory; but there is no doubt that there is a substantial part of organic chemistry which is better accounted for by pictorial orbital theory than by conventional electronic theory. Both approaches attempt to describe in qualitative terms facts which can only be fully accounted for by rigorous mathematical treatment. Chemistry has not yet reached the stage when any but the simplest reactions can be fully analyzed on the computer.

Nomenclature

We have tried to avoid the terms of the electronic theory and in general we are concerned with orbital interaction. We will, however, have occasion to describe the movement of electrons, and to classify the groups involved we will use the terms *electron repeller* in place of +I, *electron donor* in place of +R or +M, *electron attractor* in place of −I, and *electron acceptor* in place of −R or −M. The electron donors and electron acceptors involve orbitals of π-symmetry. A substituent like a halogen has electrons of π-symmetry but it is also a very electronegative atom; we can call such groups *electron attracting donors* instead of using the symbol: −I, +R. In chemical reactions involving the transfer of electrons from the Highest Occupied Molecular Orbital (HOMO) of one species to the Lowest Unoccupied Molecular Orbital (LUMO) of another species we shall call the electron donating species the HOMO-gen and the electron accepting species the LUMO-gen (Ingold, nucleophile and electrophile).

The concerted displacement reactions (see Chapter 5) we will call 'displacement reactions' and so avoid the unfortunate term S_N2 which confuses students into believing that the nucleus takes some direct part in the reaction. The term 'unimolecular ionization' will be used where appropriate in preference to the term S_N1 (see Chapter 9).

1 Atomic and Molecular Orbitals

Atoms form molecules by sharing electrons and we regard the sharing of two electrons by two atoms as constituting a chemical bond. Atoms can share one, two or three electron pairs (these correspond to single, double and triple bonds of classical valence theory). Before we can meaningfully discuss electrons in molecules we need to remind ourselves of some qualitative ideas of the arrangement of electrons in atoms.

A hydrogen atom consists of a nucleus (a proton) with an associated electron. The exact position of the electron cannot be determined; instead we can determine the probability of finding the electron at any point in space. In the case of the ground state of a hydrogen atom the probability distribution is spherical around the nucleus and it is possible to draw a spherical boundary surface inside which there is about 95 per cent probability of finding the electron. The electron has a fixed energy and a fixed spatial distribution called an *orbital*. In the helium molecule there are two electrons associated with the helium nucleus. These two electrons have exactly the same spatial distribution and hence exactly the same energy (i.e. they occupy the same orbital) but they differ in their spin (the Pauli exclusion principle). This is quite general: electrons associated with atomic nuclei occupy orbitals of fixed energy and with determined spatial distribution, and each orbital can only contain a maximum of two electrons with anti-parallel spins.

In physics, periodic phenomena are frequently associated with a 'wave equation', and in atomic theory the relevant equation is called the 'Schrödinger Equation'. The wave equation predicts discrete solutions and in one dimension for a particle confined to a box with infinite walls, the solutions can be depicted as shown in Fig. 1.1. $\psi_1 \rightarrow \psi_4$ represents solutions of increasing energy (note also increasing number of nodes). There is no direct physical interpretation of the wave function ψ, but $\psi^2 \, d\tau$ is taken to be a measure of the probability of finding an electron in a small volume of space $d\tau$ (in one dimension as shown on p. 2 for a small value dx).

In three dimensions the equation determines the energy and defines the spatial distribution of each electron. Solutions of the

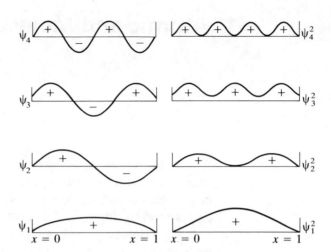

Fig. 1.1

wave equation in three dimensions enable us to calculate the 'shape' of each atomic orbital i.e. boundary surfaces inside of which there is, say, 90 per cent probability of finding the electron. Thus the first five solutions of the wave equation for an electron associated with a proton (nucleus) can be depicted as shown in Fig. 1.2.

In the hydrogen atom the 1s atomic orbital is the lowest in energy, while the remainder $(2s, 2p_x, 2p_y, 2p_z)$ are of equal energy (i.e. degenerate), but for all other atoms the 2s atomic orbital is of lower energy than the $2p_x, 2p_y, 2p_z$ orbitals which are degenerate. The figure shows ψ rather than ψ^2 because as we shall see when considering valency, the sign of the wave equation is extremely important. Further review of atomic theory need not concern us.

In atoms, electrons occupy 'atomic orbitals' of specific energy and spatial distribution. In molecules, electrons occupy similar 'molecular orbitals' which embrace the molecule. The simplest molecule is hydrogen which can be considered to be made up of two separate protons and two electrons. There are two

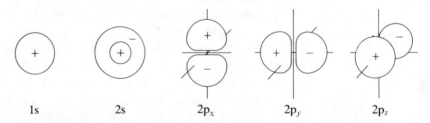

| 1s | 2s | $2p_x$ | $2p_y$ | $2p_z$ |

Fig. 1.2 The first five solutions for ψ for the wave equation. The '+' and '−' signs have the same significance as they have in Fig. 1.1

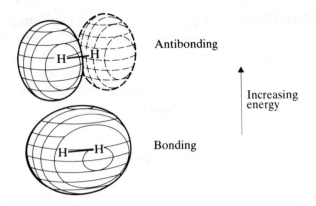

Fig. 1.3

molecular orbitals for hydrogen which can be depicted as shown
in Fig. 1.3. The lower energy orbital has its greatest electron
density between the two nuclei and a qualitative picture would
be to regard the negatively charged electrons as holding the two
positively charged nuclei together like jam in a sandwich. The
bonding molecular orbital is of lower energy than the 1s atomic
orbitals of hydrogen and is referred to as a *bonding orbital*. This
orbital is more stable than two separated atomic hydrogen
orbitals. In contrast, in the upper molecular orbital, there is a
node in the electronic wave function and the electron density is
low between the two positively charged nuclei (i.e. there is
insufficient jam to overcome the mutual repulsion of the atoms
and to hold the sandwich together). The energy of the upper
molecular orbital is greater than that of a 1s atomic orbital. Such
molecular orbitals are described as *antibonding*.

Normally the two electrons in a hydrogen molecule occupy
the bonding molecular orbital with their spins anti-parallel (i.e.
the Pauli principle applies to molecules as well as atoms). If
molecular hydrogen is irradiated by light from the far ultra-
violet region a molecule may absorb light and one of the two
electrons will be promoted to the antibonding orbital (σ^*). To a
first approximation, the energy of the electron in the antibonding orbital cancels out the effect of the electron in the bonding
orbital (σ) and the atoms can drift apart. This is not an
important way of dissociating molecular hydrogen but it can be

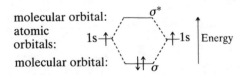

Fig. 1.4 Bonding and anti-bonding orbitals on a hydrogen molecule

very important in dissociating other molecules (for example molecular chlorine and molecular bromine are dissociated in this way). We can represent the energy levels in a hydrogen molecule by a diagram which shows how two 1s atomic orbitals combine to form two molecular orbitals, one bonding σ and one antibonding σ^* (Fig. 1.4).

Further reading

The Chemical Bond, J. H. Murrell, S. F. A. Kettle and J. M. Tedder, Wiley, Chichester, 1979.

2 Pictorial Orbital Theory

In terms of the electron pair theory (Lewis dot structure) methane consists of four hydrogens bound by four electron pairs to a central carbon atom. The innermost electrons occupying the 1s orbital of the carbon atom can be regarded as non-bonding and can be neglected for most chemical applications. There are four valence molecular orbitals in methane, but they are not identical. They consist of one orbital with no nodal plane, and three degenerate (i.e. of equal energy) orbitals, each of which contains a nodal plane. Figure 2.1 depicts the four orbitals. It is important to realize that the existence of bonding orbitals of different energy in no way conflicts with the electron pair picture in which each 'carbon–hydrogen' bond is identical. The tetrahedral disposition of the hydrogen atoms follows from the combination of the four orbitals. The only circumstance in which the presence of differing molecular orbitals is apparent is when the electron energy levels are being directly probed as in photo-electron spectroscopy. The photo-electron spectrum of methane confirms that there are two different occupied electronic levels in the valence shell of the methane molecule.

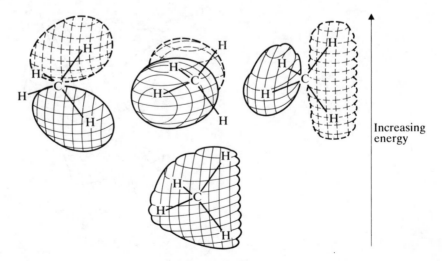

Increasing energy

Fig. 2.1 The bonding orbitals of methane

The ethane molecule has fourteen valence electrons occupying seven bonding molecular orbitals (Fig. 2.2).

The actual sign of the wave function and the presence of nodal planes is better illustrated by the pictorial diagram Fig. 2.3. Four of the molecular orbitals occur as degenerate pairs, a simplification which is not shown by the molecular orbitals of propane. (A

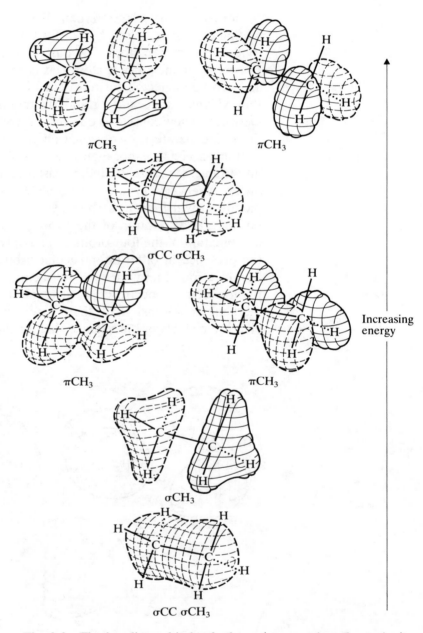

Increasing energy

Fig. 2.2 The bonding orbitals of ethane (staggered conformation)

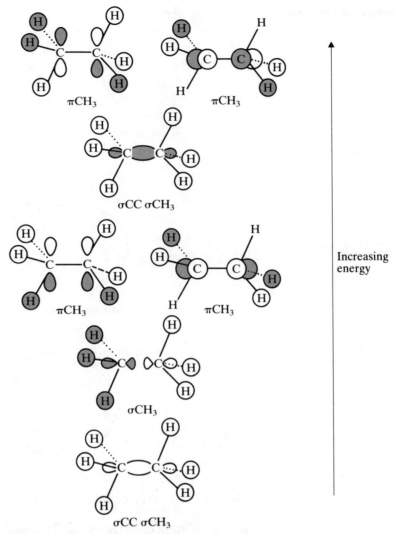

Fig. 2.3 The bonding orbitals of ethane (symmetry)

π orbital has a nodal plane containing the bond axis while a σ orbital has no nodal plane.)

In propane there are ten bonding molecular orbitals with twenty valence electrons to go in them, and although there is no degeneracy, the energies of the three highest occupied orbitals are very similar.

Molecules with lone pairs

A simple diatomic molecule with different nuclei is hydrogen fluoride (Fig. 2.4). There are eight valence electrons which go

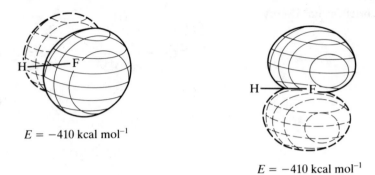

$E = -410 \text{ kcal mol}^{-1}$

$E = -410 \text{ kcal mol}^{-1}$

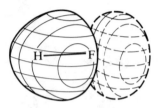

$E = -480 \text{ kcal mol}^{-1}$

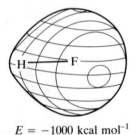

$E = -1000 \text{ kcal mol}^{-1}$

Fig. 2.4   The occupied molecular orbitals of hydrogen fluoride

into four molecular orbitals. The two orbitals with the highest energy are degenerate; they are of the π-type and have no electron density associated with the hydrogen atom, i.e. they are 'Non Bonding Orbitals' (NBO) and in Lewis Theory are represented as two 'lone pairs'. The second important difference between hydrogen fluoride and the molecules we have discussed so far is that the valence electron density is not distributed equally about the molecule. There is much greater electron density around the fluorine atom. This is because fluorine is the most electronegative of all the elements.* This means that in each bonding molecular orbital fluorine takes a larger share of the electron density.

* For a precise definition of electronegativity, see Chapter 4; for the present it can be regarded as the intrinsic property of an atom to attract electrons to itself when it is bonded.

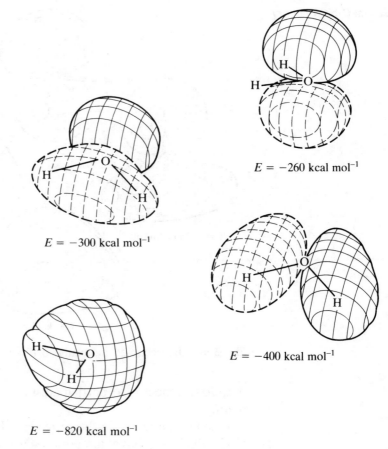

$E = -260$ kcal mol^{-1}

$E = -300$ kcal mol^{-1}

$E = -400$ kcal mol^{-1}

$E = -820$ kcal mol^{-1}

Fig. 2.5 The occupied molecular orbitals of water

In the water molecule (Fig. 2.5) there is no degeneracy, but the highest occupied orbital is non-bonding and localized on the heavy atom, oxygen, like the non-bonding orbitals of hydrogen fluoride. The next lowest orbital is also non-bonding and has a lobe pointing away from the two hydrogens corresponding to the second 'lone pair' of Lewis Theory. Again we see oxygen takes more than its 'fair share' of the total electron density. The other important feature of the water molecule is that all the bonding molecular orbitals are of higher energy than the corresponding orbitals in hydrogen fluoride.

Ammonia (Fig. 2.6) has a degenerate pair of bonding orbitals, and like hydrogen fluoride and water there is a non-bonding orbital. The highest occupied orbital has a lobe which points away from the hydrogen atoms and corresponds to the 'lone pair' of Lewis Theory. Notice that this is the molecular orbital with the highest energy of the three molecules; we shall

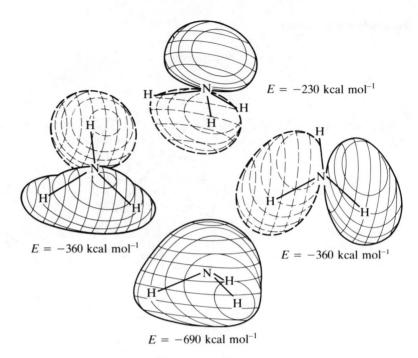

Fig. 2.6   The occupied molecular orbitals of ammonia

therefore expect it to participate in chemical reactions the most readily.

The next molecule in the series HF, H_2O and H_3N is of course H_4C which we have already discussed and which unlike the other three molecules has no non-bonding orbitals.

The highest occupied molecular orbitals in methanol and methylamine (Fig. 2.7) are non-bonding and have a spatial distribution very similar to the spatial distribution of the highest

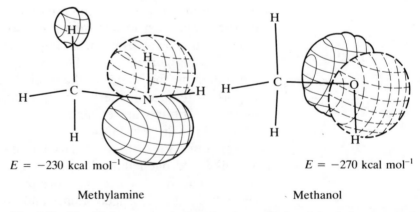

Fig. 2.7   The highest occupied molecular orbitals of methylamine and methanol

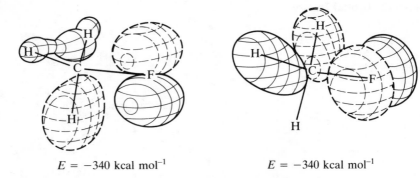

$$E = -340 \text{ kcal mol}^{-1} \qquad\qquad E = -340 \text{ kcal mol}^{-1}$$

Fig. 2.8 The highest occupied molecular orbitals (degenerate pair) of fluoromethane

occupied molecular orbitals of water and ammonia respectively. More important, the energy of the highest occupied orbital of water and methanol is almost identical ($-260 \text{ kcal mol}^{-1}$) and likewise the energies of the highest occupied orbitals of ammonia and methylamine are nearly identical. These close similarities of the 'frontier' orbitals correctly suggest that there will be a very substantial similarity in the chemical properties.

The highest occupied orbitals of fluoromethane (Fig. 2.8) are a degenerate pair like those of hydrogen fluoride. But there the similarity ends. The spatial distribution of the highest occupied orbitals of fluoromethane and hydrogen fluoride is very different. As would be expected, the energies of the degenerate pair of the fluoromethane orbitals ($-340 \text{ kcal mol}^{-1}$) are significantly different from the corresponding degenerate pair of orbitals of hydrogen fluoride ($-410 \text{ kcal mol}^{-1}$). Notice that the energies of the highest occupied orbitals of methylamine, methanol and fluoromethane are in the order $-230 > -270 \gg -340 \text{ kcal mol}^{-1}$ respectively. Thus the 'lone pair' on nitrogen in methylamine is more available for bonding that the highest non-bonded pair on oxygen in methanol (methylamine is a strong base, methanol a weak one). In contrast the non-bonded electron pairs in fluoromethane take no part in normal bonding.

Molecules with double bonds

In molecules in which the number of bonding electron pairs exceeds the number of unions between atoms, the extra electrons occupy molecular orbitals which are generally of higher energy than those molecules in which the number of bonding pairs of electrons equals the number of unions, i.e. these higher energy orbitals are the double bonds of classical

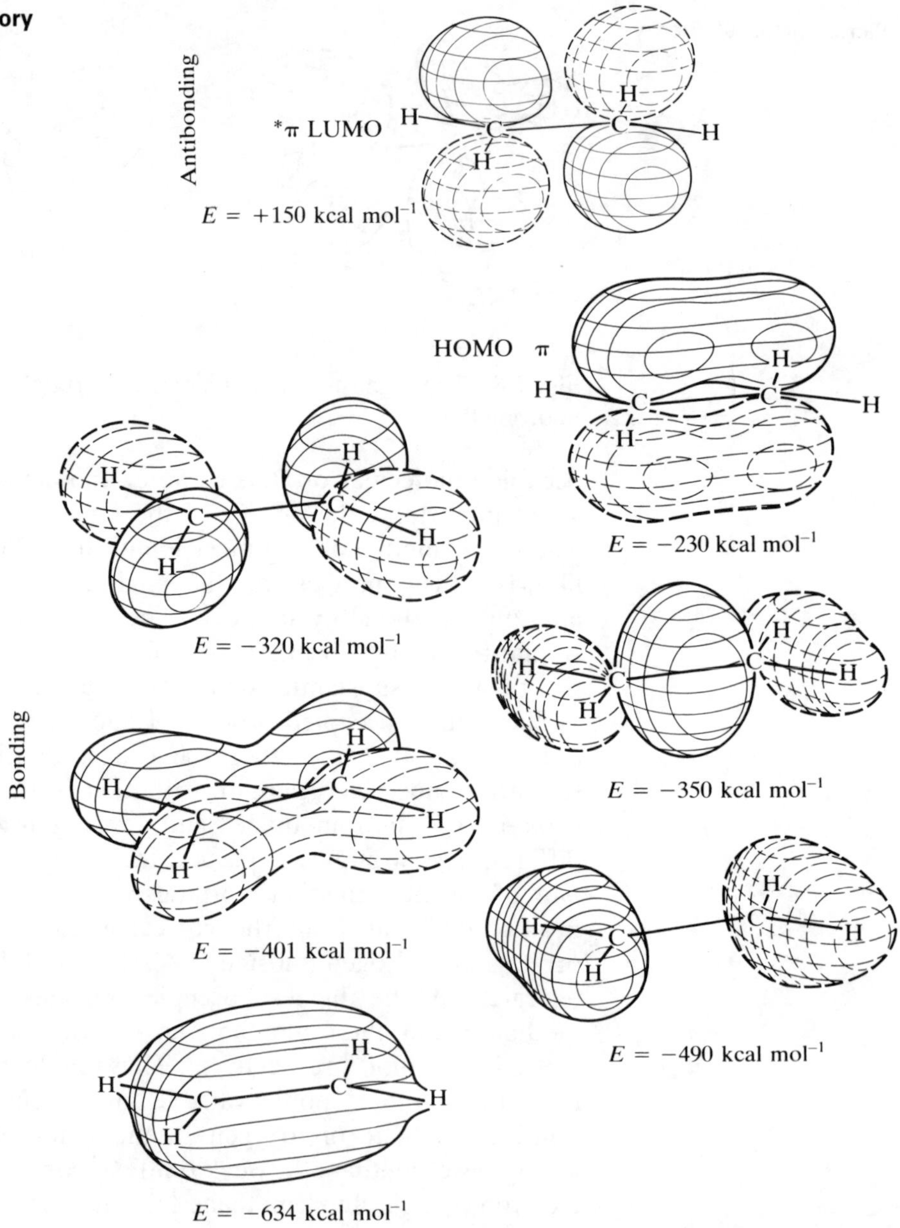

Antibonding

*π LUMO

$E = +150 \text{ kcal mol}^{-1}$

HOMO π

$E = -230 \text{ kcal mol}^{-1}$

$E = -320 \text{ kcal mol}^{-1}$

$E = -350 \text{ kcal mol}^{-1}$

Bonding

$E = -401 \text{ kcal mol}^{-1}$

$E = -490 \text{ kcal mol}^{-1}$

$E = -634 \text{ kcal mol}^{-1}$

Fig. 2.9 The bonding orbitals of ethene

electronic structure theory. These orbitals have a local nodal plane containing the atoms sharing in these π-type orbitals. At first we will only consider molecules with one 'double bond' (e.g. alkenes and carbonyl compounds).

The simplest alkene is ethene and its bonding molecular orbitals together with the lowest unoccupied orbital are shown (Fig. 2.9). As we shall see (Chapter 7) the chemistry of ethene is dominated by the two 'frontier orbitals', that is the *highest occupied molecular orbital* (HOMO) and the *lowest unoccupied molecular orbital* (LUMO). Figure 2.10 shows the frontier orbitals of propene. Notice that the frontier orbitals of propene are associated with the carbon atoms sharing four electrons. There is very little electron density associated with the CH_3-group and the HOMO and LUMO are very similar to the corresponding orbitals in ethene.

When the 'double bond' is associated with a heteroatom (i.e. other than carbon) the molecular orbitals are affected depending on the intrinsic electron attraction of the heteroatom, i.e. the relative electronegativity (cf. the orbitals of HF and water). The simplest compound with a 'double bond' and a heteroatom is formaldehyde (Fig. 2.11). Notice that one of the non-bonding 'lone pairs' on the oxygen occupies the HOMO. The second pair of non-bonding electrons occupies an orbital (not shown) of lower energy than the 'π-orbital'.

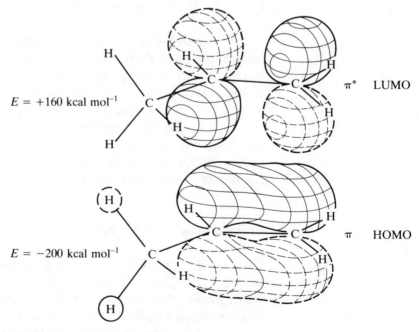

$E = +160 \text{ kcal mol}^{-1}$ π^* LUMO

$E = -200 \text{ kcal mol}^{-1}$ π HOMO

Fig. 2.10 The frontier orbitals of propene

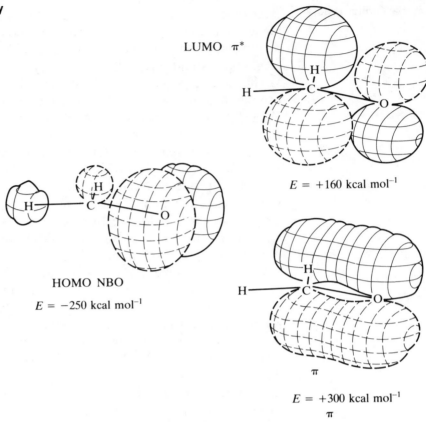

LUMO π^*

$E = +160$ kcal mol^{-1}

HOMO NBO

$E = -250$ kcal mol^{-1}

π

$E = +300$ kcal mol^{-1}

π

Fig. 2.11 The frontier orbitals of formaldehyde

The frontier orbitals of acetaldehyde (Fig. 2.12) are very similar indeed to those of formaldehyde, in accordance with the concept of functional group (in this case the carbonyl group).

The frontier orbitals of acetone (Fig. 2.13) are likewise very similar to formaldehyde and acetaldehyde.

Classical organic chemistry was built up on the concept of functional groups. We can see that the presence of a functional group (in the present case the carbonyl group) corresponds to the possession of a particular orbital arrangement.

Molecules with triple bonds

The bonding molecular orbitals of acetylene (ethyne) are shown in Fig. 2.14. The highest occupied orbitals are a degenerate pair. Notice that they are of lower energy than the HOMO of ethene and therefore are less available for reaction.

The replacement of one of the hydrogen atoms by a methyl

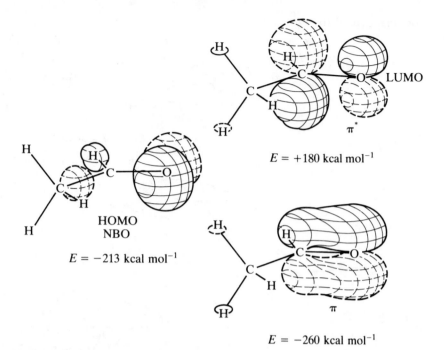

$E = +180 \text{ kcal mol}^{-1}$

π^*

LUMO

HOMO
NBO

$E = -213 \text{ kcal mol}^{-1}$

π

$E = -260 \text{ kcal mol}^{-1}$

Fig. 2.12   The frontier orbitals of acetaldehyde

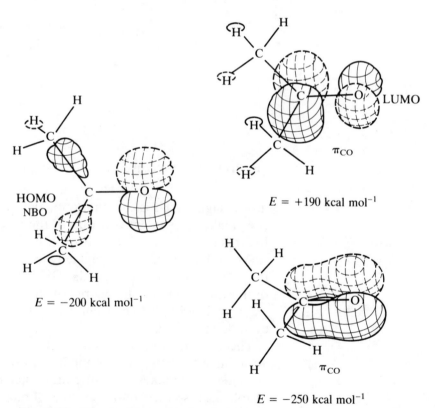

π_{CO}

LUMO

$E = +190 \text{ kcal mol}^{-1}$

HOMO
NBO

$E = -200 \text{ kcal mol}^{-1}$

π_{CO}

$E = -250 \text{ kcal mol}^{-1}$

Fig. 2.13   The frontier orbitals of acetone

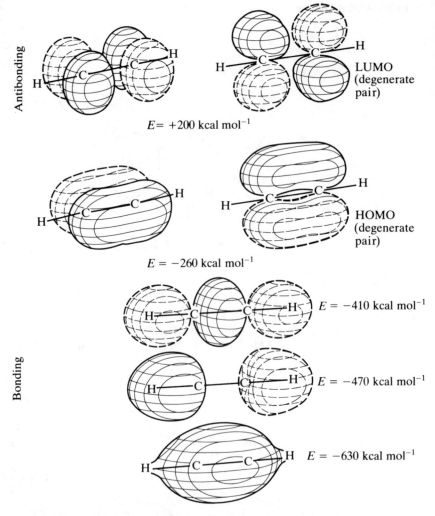

Fig. 2.14 The molecular orbitals of acetylene (ethyne)

group slightly raises the energy of the degenerate HOMO pair (i.e. makes less negative), due to the interaction of the methyl hydrogens with the π-orbitals (Fig. 2.15).

As we have seen for formaldehyde, a heteroatom affects both the energy and the charge distribution of a π-type molecular orbital; for example the energy of the HOMO (pair) goes from -260 kcal mol^{-1} for acetylene to -300 kcal mol^{-1} for hydrogen cyanide (Fig. 2.16).

The introduction of a methyl group in place of a hydrogen atom in ethene to give propene (or in formaldehyde to give acetaldehyde) makes very little difference to the frontier orbitals (Table 2.1); so the frontier orbitals of methyl cyanide (Fig. 2.17) are similar to hydrogen cyanide.

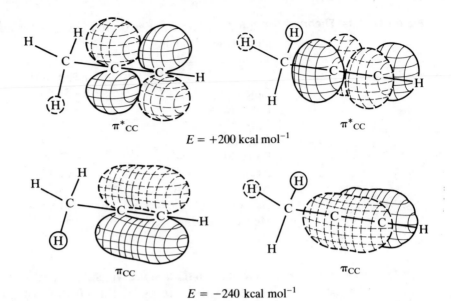

Fig. 2.15 The degenerate HOMO and LUMO pairs of methyl acetylene (propyne) (CH$_3$C≡CH)

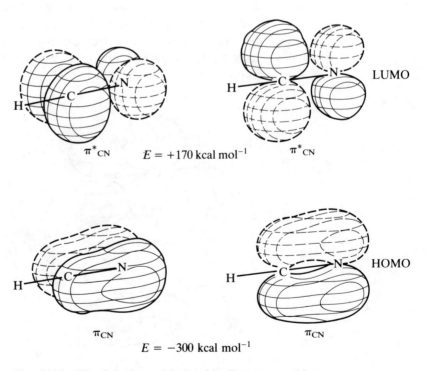

Fig. 2.16 The frontier orbitals of hydrogen cyanide

Table 2.1 The frontier orbital energies for alkenes, alkynes, ketones and nitriles, kcal mol^{-1}

	π(HOMO)	π^*(LUMO)
Ethene $=$	−54.96	+35.84
Propene$=$	−47.79	+38.23
Ethyne $\equiv$	−62.12	+47.79
Propyne$\equiv$	−59.74	+47.79
Formaldehyde$=$O	−71.68	+38.23
Acetaldehyde $=$O	−62.13	+43.01
Acetone $=$O	−59.74	+45.40
Hydrogen cyanide$\equiv$N	−71.68	+40.62
Methyl cyanide $\equiv$N	−59.74	+54.96

Notice that a methyl substituent raises (i.e. makes less negative) the energy of the HOMO of an adjacent double (or triple) bond; and a methyl substituent raises (i.e. makes more positive) the energy of the LUMO of an adjacent double (or triple) bond. We shall see later that this means that the methyl substituent will render the adjacent double (or triple) bond more susceptible to attack by a LUMO-gen (e.g. a proton) but less susceptible to attack by a HOMO-gen (e.g. an alkoxide anion). It is *not* valid to compare the reactivity of different classes of molecule, e.g. an alkene with a ketone, in terms of frontier orbitals alone, because this is only one factor and other factors, for example changes in polarity, can be particularly important.

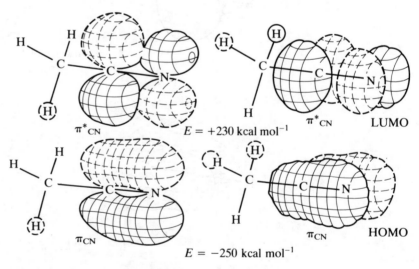

Fig. 2.17 The frontier orbitals of methyl cyanide

Allyl and molecules of the type $\ddot{X}$—Y=Z

The carbon π-type orbitals of ethene and similar molecules can extend over more than two atoms. The simplest example, the allyl cation (Fig. 2.18), has three molecular orbitals of this type corresponding to the three carbon atoms which are incorporated. In the cation only the lowest 'π_1' orbital is

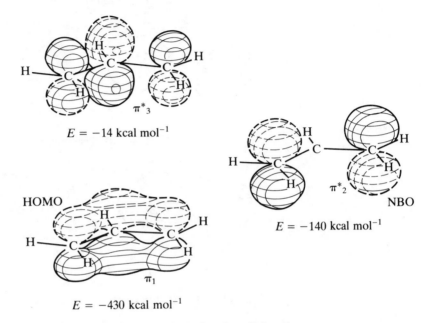

$$E = -14 \text{ kcal mol}^{-1}$$

$$E = -140 \text{ kcal mol}^{-1}$$

$$E = -430 \text{ kcal mol}^{-1}$$

Fig. 2.18 The frontier orbitals for the allyl cation

occupied. The second 'π_2' orbital contains one electron in the allyl radical and two electrons in the allyl anion; this is a Non Bonding Orbital (NBO). The uppermost 'π_3' orbital is unoccupied in the ground state of the cation, radical or anion but we have included it so that the relationship between allyl orbitals and those of carbon dioxide and other carbonyl compounds can be appreciated.

Carbon dioxide is the simplest symmetrical neutral molecule which has π-type orbitals over three atoms (Fig. 2.19).

The frontier orbitals are further apart than the other examples of the allyl type molecule, i.e. the HOMO is of lower energy and takes little part in initiating reactions. In conformity carbon dioxide is unreactive, only undergoing attack at the central atom by powerful electron donors (see later).

The frontier orbitals of formyl fluoride (Fig. 2.20) and formamide (Fig. 2.21) are interesting. The difference in

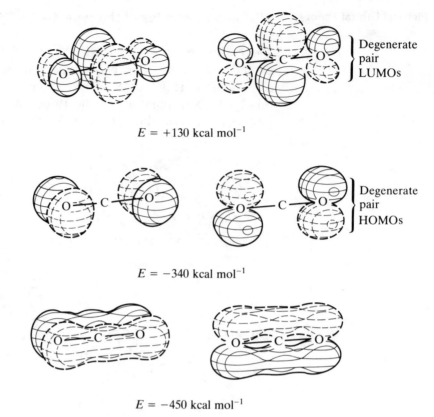

$E = +130$ kcal mol^{-1}

$E = -340$ kcal mol^{-1}

$E = -450$ kcal mol^{-1}

Fig. 2.19 The frontier orbitals of carbon dioxide

electronegativity of the fluorine atom and the NH_2 group not only affects the spatial distribution of the orbitals but also their order. Thus the 'π_3' orbital is the LUMO for both formamide and formyl fluoride, but the 'π_2' orbital is the HOMO for formamide while the non-bonding orbital centred on the oxygen is the HOMO for formyl fluoride.

Butadiene, acrolein and longer conjugated chains

By analogy with allyl which has three π-type orbitals extended over three carbon atoms we would expect four π-type orbitals extended over all four carbon atoms in 1,3-butadiene. However, unlike allyl which must exist as a cation, radical or anion, 1,3-butadiene (Fig. 2.22) is a stable neutral molecule.

The orbitals in acrolein (Fig. 2.23) are basically similar though just as the heteroatoms in formyl fluoride and formamide introduce additional non-bonding orbitals, so the oxygen in

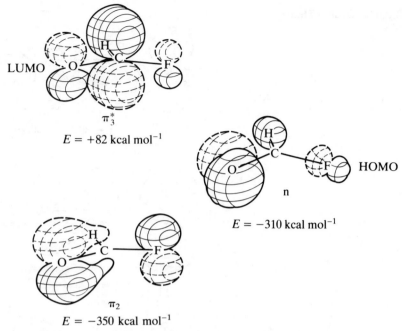

LUMO

π_3^*

$E = +82\ \text{kcal mol}^{-1}$

HOMO

n

$E = -310\ \text{kcal mol}^{-1}$

π_2

$E = -350\ \text{kcal mol}^{-1}$

Fig. 2.20　The frontier orbitals of formyl fluoride

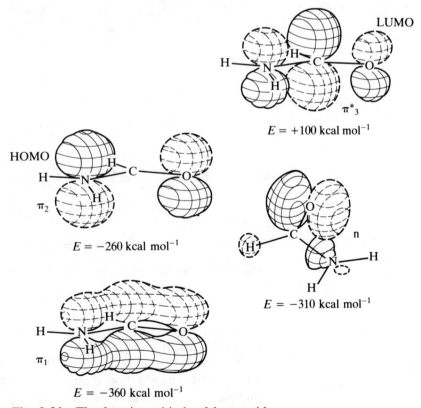

LUMO

π_3^*

$E = +100\ \text{kcal mol}^{-1}$

HOMO

π_2

$E = -260\ \text{kcal mol}^{-1}$

n

$E = -310\ \text{kcal mol}^{-1}$

π_1

$E = -360\ \text{kcal mol}^{-1}$

Fig. 2.21　The frontier orbitals of formamide

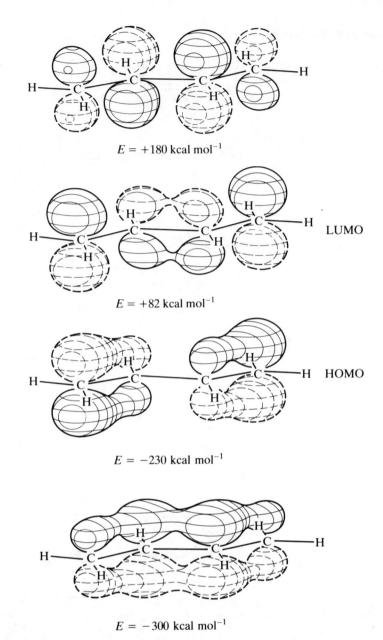

$E = +180 \text{ kcal mol}^{-1}$

$E = +82 \text{ kcal mol}^{-1}$ LUMO

$E = -230 \text{ kcal mol}^{-1}$ HOMO

$E = -300 \text{ kcal mol}^{-1}$

Fig. 2.22 The $\pi(\text{C—C})$ orbitals of butadiene (transoid)

acrolein introduces two additional non-bonding orbitals, the upper one being the HOMO.

We shall see in Chapter 10 that the extension of the delocalized $\pi(\text{C—C})$ orbitals to cyclic compounds is very important.

This chapter has described the orbitals of a variety of types of

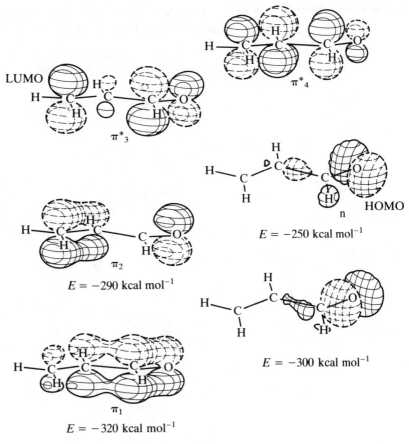

Fig. 2.23 The π orbitals of acrolein

molecule; the remainder of the book will discuss chemical reactions in terms of the interaction of molecular orbitals.

Further reading

The Organic Chemist's Book of Orbitals, W. J. Jorgensen and L. Salem, Academic Press, New York, 1973.

Problems

1   Depict the HOMO of dimethyl ether.

2   Draw the frontier orbitals of ethene and formaldehyde. Comment on their similarities and differences.

3 Draw the π-orbitals for the hypothetical molecule trimethylene methane $(CH_2)_3C$.

4 Compare the frontier orbitals of formamide and formyl fluoride and explain the relative orbital energies.

3 Hybridization and Group Orbitals

We saw, in Chapter 2, that methane contained two types of bonding molecular orbital, a totally symmetric ψ_1 and three degenerate orbitals ψ_2, ψ_3 and ψ_4, each containing a nodal plane. This does not mean that there is any difference in the bonding of the four hydrogen atoms. The hydrogen atoms are arranged tetrahedrally around the central carbon atom and the 'bonds' are of equal energy. To calculate the bond dissociation energy and other physical characteristics of the carbon-hydrogen bonds it is convenient to combine the 2s and the three 2p carbon atomic orbitals and so obtain hybrid orbitals sp^3 (the symbol sp^3 indicating that the hybrid is made up from one 2s and three 2p atomic orbitals). These hybrid carbon orbitals overlap with the four hydrogen 1s atomic orbitals to form the four tetrahedral bonds. Hybridization is a mathematical technique which enables us to calculate the energy and spatial orientation of atoms in a molecule. If we study the energy levels in methane by a technique such as photoelectron spectroscopy we find that there are indeed two energy levels as depicted in Chapter 2. On the other hand, the value of the H—^{13}C nmr coupling constant can be interpreted in terms of the s character of the carbon orbital.

The energy levels and electron densities in ethene are shown in Chapter 2 (page 12). There are six bonding orbitals, all of slightly differing energy. We can alternatively regard the ethene molecule (Fig. 3.1) as built up of sp^2 hybrid orbitals of the two carbon atoms which overlap with each other and with

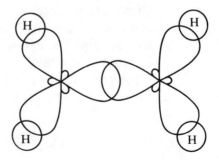

Fig. 3.1 The overlapping of sp^2 hybrid orbitals to form five 'single' bonds in ethene

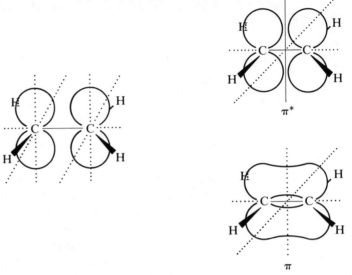

Fig. 3.2 The $2p_z$ atomic orbitals, perpendicular to the plane containing the hybrid orbitals, which combine to form π-orbitals in ethene

the 1s atomic orbitals of the hydrogen atoms (the symbol sp^2 indicating that the hybrid is made up from one 2s and two 2p atomic orbitals). The five hybrid molecular orbitals lie in the same plane subtending from each carbon atom an angle of 120° to each other, and each of these molecular orbitals contains two electrons. This leaves a non-bonded electron on each carbon atom in two 2p atomic orbitals not contributing to the hybrids (Fig. 3.2). These orbitals are perpendicular to the plane containing the hybrid orbitals. Overlap of these $2p_z$ atomic orbitals will lead to molecular orbitals which correspond exactly to the HOMO(π) and LUMO(π^*) depicted in Chapter 2.

The energy levels and electron densities in acetylene (ethyne) are shown in Chapter 2 (page 16). There are five occupied bonding orbitals, the two uppermost of which are degenerate. We can alternatively regard the acetylene molecule as containing orbitals made up from sp atomic orbitals of carbon (the symbol sp indicating the hybrid orbital is made up from one 2s and one 2p atomic orbitals). These hybrid orbitals overlap with each other and with two 1s atomic orbitals of the hydrogen atoms to form a linear molecule (Fig. 3.3). This arrangement leaves each

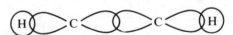

Fig. 3.3 The overlapping sp hybrid orbitals forming the three 'single' bonds in acetylene

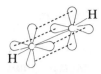

Fig. 3.4   sp Hybrid bonds in acetylene together with the $2p_y$ and $2p_z$ atomic orbitals which combine to form two orthogonal π orbitals

carbon atom with two 2p atomic orbitals $(2p_y; 2p_z)$ each containing one electron which do not contribute to the hybrid overlaps (Fig. 3.4). Overlap of these two pairs of 2p atomic orbitals leads to four molecular orbitals identical to the HOMO and LUMO degenerate pair depicted in Chapter 2.

On page 13 we show the frontier orbitals of propene. Comparison of these orbitals with those of ethene (page 12) shows that they have very similar shape and very similar energies. The same is true if we compare the frontier orbitals of propyne (page 17) with those of acetylene itself (page 16). This provides some justification for the 'functional group' concept of organic chemistry. Another example is the carbonyl group. The frontier orbitals of formaldehyde, acetaldehyde and acetone are shown on pages 14 and 15). The similarity of the shapes and energies is very manifest.

Hybrid orbitals preserve the concepts of a functional group and localized bonds. However hybridization no more represents a physical phenomenon than resonance between different structures is a physical phenomenon. It will also be clear that the carbonyl group in formaldehyde, though similar, is not identical in energy or spatial characteristics with the carbonyl group in acetaldehyde. In acetaldehyde there is some electron density of the π orbital on the hydrogen atoms of the methyl group. The same extended distribution of π orbitals occurs with the HOMO of propene and the degenerate HOMOs of propyne. Nonetheless the striking feature of the three carbonyl groups we have discussed is their similarity.

The concept of an electron pair bond is of such value to organic chemistry that hybridization forms a very useful intellectual bridge between simple structural ideas and molecular orbital ideas.

Further reading

The Chemical Bond, Chapter 8, J. H. Murrell, S. F. A. Kettle and J. M. Tedder, Wiley, Chichester, 1979.

Problem

Draw the appropriate hybrid orbitals of formaldehyde and compare them with the frontier orbitals of formaldehyde.

4 The Carbon–Hydrogen Bond and Radical Transfer Reactions

If we consider a molecule AB, where the two atoms A and B are bound together by sharing a pair of electrons, the bond between A and B can break in three ways as depicted in the following diagram:

$$A{:}B \longrightarrow A^+ + {:}B^-$$
$$A{:}B \longrightarrow A{:}^- + B^+ \Big\} \text{ Heterolysis, giving ions}$$

$$A{:}B \longrightarrow A{\cdot} + B{\cdot} \quad \text{Homolysis, giving free radicals}$$

The C–H bond in alkanes is nonpolar and does not readily undergo ionic reactions. It does, however, readily undergo free radical reactions.

The simplest chemical reaction is that of a hydrogen atom with a hydrogen molecule. Very similar is the reaction of methyl

$$H{\cdot} + H_2 \longrightarrow H_2 + H{\cdot} \quad (\log A = 10.7\,\mathrm{l\,mol^{-1}\,s^{-1}}$$
$$E_{act} = 9.4\,\mathrm{kcal\,mol^{-1}}) \quad (1)$$

radicals with methane. The large difference in the pre-exponential terms

$$CH_3{\cdot} + CH_4 \longrightarrow CH_4 + CH_3{\cdot} \quad (\log A = 8.8\,\mathrm{l\,mol^{-1}\,s^{-1}}$$
$$E_{act} = 14.2\,\mathrm{kcal\,mol^{-1}}) \quad (2)$$

is due to the loss of rotational entropy in the transition state for reaction (2).

The important features of the carbon–hydrogen bond are its non-polar characteristics and its relatively high bond dissociation energy $D(CH_3{-}H) = 104\,\mathrm{kcal\,mol^{-1}}$. The alkanes are often described as unreactive but in fact it depends entirely on the nature of the reaction under consideration. Methane does not react under normal conditions with either sulfuric acid or sodium hydroxide, but in the presence of light it reacts rapidly with chlorine and, once the reaction is initiated, explosively with oxygen. These latter reactions involve methyl radicals and in general, alkanes which are inert towards reagents with complete shells react rapidly with reagents with open shells, e.g. $CH_3{\cdot}$ or CH_3^+. Free methyl cations are so reactive that they are normally studied in the vapour phase in a mass spectrometer. Methyl radicals are also very reactive and can never exist in high concentration because two radicals on collision will combine (to yield ethane).

The weakest bonds in alkanes are the carbon–carbon bonds and yet the reactions of atoms and radicals with aliphatic hydrocarbons involve, almost exclusively, the fission of carbon–hydrogen bonds. This is because the carbon chain in an alkane is completely encased by carbon–hydrogen bonds and for steric reasons an attacking atom or radical will form a new bond with a hydrogen rather than a carbon atom. It does not mean that all attacking reagents always attack hydrogen atoms in preference to carbon. The reactions of ionic reagents for example are more often governed by polar rather than by steric effects.

Some common examples of radical reactions include:

$$CH_3\cdot + C_2H_6 \longrightarrow CH_4 + C_2H_5\cdot$$
$$Cl\cdot \;\; + C_2H_6 \longrightarrow HCl + C_2H_5\cdot$$
$$HO\cdot \;\; + C_2H_6 \longrightarrow H_2O + C_2H_5\cdot$$

All these reactions are fast, and because the common product in these reactions is an ethyl radical which is also a very reactive species, many radical reactions involve a chain reaction. The chlorination of methane provides a good example of a chain process. The reaction is initiated by light (or heat) through the homolysis of a chlorine–chlorine bond.

$$Cl_2 \longrightarrow 2Cl\cdot \qquad\qquad \text{Initiation}$$

$$\left.\begin{array}{l} Cl\cdot \;\; + CH_4 \longrightarrow HCl \;\; + CH_3\cdot \\ CH_3\cdot + Cl_2 \longrightarrow CH_3Cl + Cl\cdot \end{array}\right\} \text{Propagation}$$

It would appear that one photon could convert a large amount of methane and chlorine into chloromethane and this is so. The propagating cycle may be repeated 10^6 times before a 'chain' termination process intervenes.

$$\left.\begin{array}{l} Cl\cdot + CH_3\cdot \longrightarrow CH_3Cl \\ CH_3\cdot + CH_3\cdot \longrightarrow C_2H_6 \\ Cl\cdot + Cl\cdot + M \longrightarrow Cl_2 + M \end{array}\right\} \text{Termination}$$

The chain termination reactions are all very fast (faster than the chain propagating steps) but the concentrations of atoms and radicals are so low that the chains in chlorination are very long. Most chain reactions are much shorter.

The principal reaction between a radical and an alkane involves the Singly Occupied Molecular Orbital (SOMO) of the

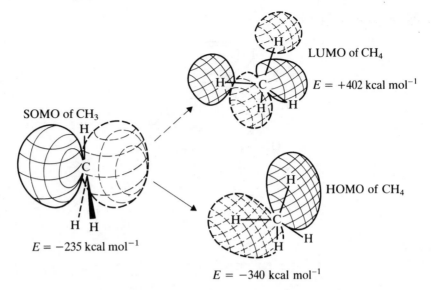

SOMO of CH_3

$E = -235 \text{ kcal mol}^{-1}$

LUMO of CH_4

$E = +402 \text{ kcal mol}^{-1}$

HOMO of CH_4

$E = -340 \text{ kcal mol}^{-1}$

Fig. 4.1 Interaction of a methyl radical with a methane molecule (not a scale drawing)

radical. The simplest radical reaction we can depict is that of methyl radicals with methane (Fig. 4.1). The SOMO can donate or accept a single electron so that both the HOMO and the LUMO of methane could be involved. The energy level of the SOMO of the radical and the HOMO of methane are close and this represents the principle interaction. The SOMO of the ethyl radical (Fig. 4.2) is similar to that of the methyl radical, although as expected the unpaired electron is more delocalized and the energy gap between the SOMO of the radical and the HOMO of ethane is slightly less, i.e. the ethyl radical is less reactive than the methyl radical.

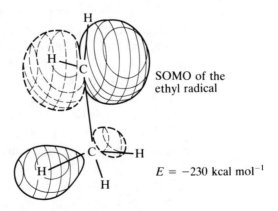

SOMO of the
ethyl radical

$E = -230 \text{ kcal mol}^{-1}$

Fig. 4.2 SOMO of the ethyl radical

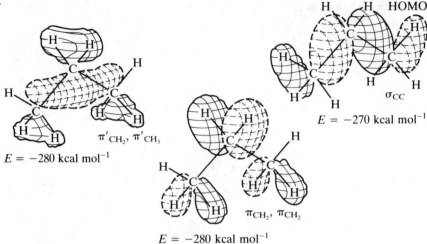

π'_{CH_2}, π'_{CH_3}

$E = -280 \text{ kcal mol}^{-1}$

σ_{CC}

$E = -270 \text{ kcal mol}^{-1}$

π_{CH_2}, π_{CH_2}

$E = -280 \text{ kcal mol}^{-1}$

Fig. 4.3   The upper occupied molecular orbitals of propane

Hydrogen abstraction by an alkyl radical from methane or ethane (see page 33) involves interaction of the SOMO of the radical with one of the upper occupied molecular orbitals of the alkane. In propane and linear alkanes the HOMO is largely associated with the bonding between carbon atoms, but access of the half filled orbital of the radical to this σ_{C-C} type orbital is greatly restricted (see Fig. 4.3). In contrast, the next two orbitals in propane are almost degenerate and their greatest electron density is associated with the hydrogen atoms attached to the central carbon atom. Thus free radical attack occurs at the hydrogens attached to the central carbon atom.

The site of hydrogen abstraction from an alkane by an alkyl radical is governed by the relative strengths of the bonds being broken and formed. These in turn are largely determined by the release of steric compression associated with the abstraction of a hydrogen atom. The activation energy for hydrogen abstraction by methyl radicals from simple alkanes is shown in Table 4.1, and it can be seen that the more crowded the site the easier hydrogen abstraction becomes.

The essential feature of these hydrogen atom transfer reactions is that polar forces are negligible. This is in very sharp contrast to hydrogen abstraction from an alkane by chlorine atoms (Table 4.2). The rate of the chlorine atom reaction is faster partly due to the large pre-exponential term but notice that both the forward and backward reactions involving chlorine have activation energies more than 10 kcal mol^{-1} lower than the corresponding reaction involving methyl. This is because the

Table 4.1 Activation parameters for H-abstraction by methyl radicals

Alkane	$\log A$ $(1\,mol^{-1}\,s^{-1})$	E_a $[kcal\,mol^{-1}]$	$\log k^{164°}$ $(1\,mol^{-1}\,s^{-1})$
CH_4	8.76	14.2	1.65
C_2H_6	8.83	11.8	2.96
$(CH_3)_2\overset{*}{C}H_2$	8.82	10.1	3.75
$(CH_3)_3\overset{*}{C}H$	8.38	8.0	4.36

* site of attack

Table 4.2 Activation energies for hydrogen atom transfer involving polar and non-polar transition states (E in kcal mol^{-1})

	E_1	E_{-1}	ΔH
$CH_3\cdot + CH_4 \underset{k_{-1}}{\overset{k_1}{\rightleftharpoons}} CH_4 + CH_3\cdot$	14.2	14.2	0
$CH_3\cdot + HCl \underset{k_{-1}}{\overset{k_1}{\rightleftharpoons}} CH_4 + Cl\cdot$	2.5	3.5	1

transition state is polar, the polarity lowering the height of the energy barrier.

$$CH_3\cdot + H{-}Cl \longrightarrow [\overrightarrow{CH_3}\cdots H\cdots \overrightarrow{Cl}] \longrightarrow CH_4 + Cl\cdot$$
$$\text{polar activated complex}$$

Polarity is a precise concept in physics, but it is not possible to completely separate polarity from other forces present in molecular structure. Electronegativity χ is necessarily a qualitative concept defined by the simple equation

$$\chi = \text{const}\,(I_A + A_A)$$

where I_A is the ionization potential of atom A and A_A is the electron affinity of atom A. If $D(A{-}A)$ is the bond dissociation energy of the molecule A_2 and $D(B{-}B)$ is the bond dissociation energy of the molecule B_2 then the bond dissociation energy of A—B, i.e. $D(A{-}B)$, will always be greater than the average of $D(A{-}A)$ and $D(B{-}B)$. This is because of polarity, attributable to the electronegativity difference of A and B.

Alkanes are unreactive towards reagents which participate in reactions involving the transfer of electron pairs, but react readily with many reagents containing unpaired electrons (e.g. radicals, halogen atoms, molecular oxygen, etc.). Although reactions of alkanes with hydrogen atoms and alkyl radicals involve non-polar transition states, reactions involving halogen atoms or with substituted alkanes can involve very polar transition states in which polarity may determine the regioselectivity of a hydrogen atom transfer reaction (Table 4.3).

Table 4.3 Hydrogen abstraction from CH_4 and CF_3H by $CH_3\cdot$ (non-polar) and $Br\cdot$ (polar)

$(\log A \text{ in } l\,mol^{-1}\,s^{-1})$ $\qquad\qquad$ $(E \text{ in kcal mol}^{-1})$

	Br·		CH₃·	
	$\log A$	E	$\log A$	E
CH_3—H	11.0	18.6	8.8	14.2
CF_3—H	10.1	22.3	7.4	13.6

Notice that the replacement of CH_3— by CF_3— increases the transition state barrier for hydrogen abstraction by bromine atoms, but slightly reduces the activation energy for abstraction by methyl radicals. In the former reaction the strong polar forces are in opposition to hydrogen abstraction while in the latter reaction the weak polar forces facilitate hydrogen abstraction.

Further reading

Radicals, D. C. Nonhebel, J. M. Tedder and J. C. Walton, Cambridge University Press, Cambridge, 1979.
Frontier Orbitals and Chemical Reactions, Chapter 5, I. Fleming, Wiley, Chichester, 1976.

Problems

1 The following activation energies were determined for hydrogen abstraction by $CH_3\cdot$ and $CF_3\cdot$ radicals. Account for the trends observed in the experimental data.

Activation energies (kcal mol^{-1})

Radical	SiH_4	$(CH_3)_3SiH$	Cl_3SiH
$CH_3\cdot$	6.9	7.8	4.3
$CF_3\cdot$	5.1	5.6	6.0

2 Compare hydrogen abstraction by Br·, CH$_3$· and CF$_3$·.

H—H H—CH$_3$ H—CH$_2$CH$_3$ H—CH(CH$_3$)$_2$ H—C(CH$_3$)$_3$

$\log k_{\text{Br}\cdot}/k_{\text{CH}_3\cdot}$

164°   −2.4   −0.5   +1.3   +1.9   +2.25

$\log k_{\text{CF}_3\cdot}/k_{\text{CH}_3\cdot}$

164°   +1.7   +1.5   +2.0   +1.1   +1.2

Account for the very large change in the relative rates ($k_{\text{Br}\cdot}/k_{\text{CH}_3\cdot}$) for hydrogen abstraction by bromination.

5 The Displacement Reaction and the Carbon–Halogen Bond

A very large class of chemical reactions involves the rearrangement of electron pairs between the reacting species. This class can be subdivided into (I) those reactions in which a pair of electrons is transferred from one reactant molecule (the donor) to the other molecule (the acceptor), and (II) those reactions which involve no net transfer of electrons but an interchange of electron pairs (pericyclic reactions). See Fig. 5.1.

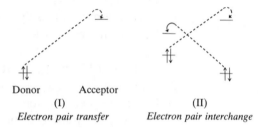

Donor   Acceptor

(I)   (II)

Electron pair transfer   *Electron pair interchange*

Fig. 5.1

This chapter is concerned with class (I), i.e. reactions in which there is a net transfer of electrons.

In general these reactions are controlled by three factors: (i) orbital interaction, (ii) Coulombic interaction, and (iii) steric requirements. In solution there is a fourth factor, 'solvation', but although solvation is a major factor in the kind of reactions we shall deal with, it is usually relatively constant for similar reactions. Steric requirements embrace effects which influence both orbital interaction and Coulombic interaction, and will be referred to later in much greater detail with reference to specific examples. At present we are concerned with 'orbital control' and 'charge (or Coulombic) control'. The charge control term will be large when there is a large energy gap between the orbitals of the donor and those of the acceptor. In contrast the orbital interaction will be large when the energy of the highest filled orbital of the donor is very close to the energy of the lowest vacant orbital of the acceptor. These are called the *frontier orbitals* (Fig. 5.2).

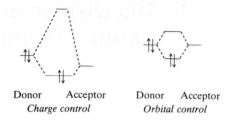

Donor	Acceptor	Donor	Acceptor
Charge control		*Orbital control*	

Fig. 5.2

Charge control is associated with a large electrostatic force between the donor and the acceptor (this does not necessarily mean either species is charged, although in many cases one of them is). Orbital control is associated with exchange between degenerate or almost degenerate pairs of orbitals. There is no sharp distinction between reactions which are orbital controlled and reactions which are charge controlled. Reactions are known which are almost entirely dependent on electrostatic interaction and there are others in which little or no charge separation is present in the transition state. In many reactions there is some separation of charge but often this polarity is not the determining factor. Just as a reaction may be 'charge controlled' and yet involve no charged species, so 'orbital controlled' reactions may involve ionic species. In general 'charge control' occurs when the charge is very localized, while in 'orbital controlled' reactions charge, if present, is diffuse. Species where the charge is localized are called *hard* while species where the charge is diffuse are called *soft*.

One of the most important reactions in organic chemistry is the '*concerted displacement reaction*'* in which a species with a non-bonded pair of electrons reacts with a neutral molecule and in a concerted process displaces an atom, ion or group. Such reactions are orbital controlled. A common example is the reaction of the hydroxide ion with an alkyl halide:

$$HO^- + CH_3Br \longrightarrow CH_3OH + Br^-$$

The attacking species can be a neutral molecule so long as it has a non-bonded pair of electrons in the highest occupied orbital (HOMO) whose energy is close to the lowest unoccupied orbital (LUMO) of the alkyl halide. Thus the reaction between ammonia and chloromethane can be regarded as a typical displacement reaction; the movements of electron pairs can be

---

* See introduction for the definition of a displacement reaction.

depicted by the use of curved arrows:

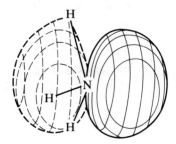

The bonding orbitals of ammonia are shown on page 00; we are at present only concerned with the HOMO (Fig. 5.3) and we can call ammonia the HOMO-gen (i.e. the species providing the HOMO).

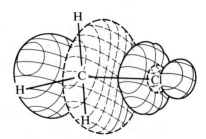

Fig. 5.3 ψ_4 HOMO of ammonia

The lowest unoccupied molecular orbital of chloromethane is shown in Fig. 5.4.

Fig. 5.4 LUMO of chloromethane σ^*C—Cl

and chloromethane is the LUMO-gen (i.e. the species providing the LUMO). We can depict the reaction as involving the overlapping of the large lobe of the HOMO of the ammonia molecule with the largest available lobe of the LUMO of the chloromethane molecule (Fig. 5.5). An important feature of this approach is that clearly the rate determining step involves one molecule of ammonia and one molecule of chloromethane, i.e. the reaction is bimolecular. Equally important is the requirement that the reaction involves inversion at the carbon atom.

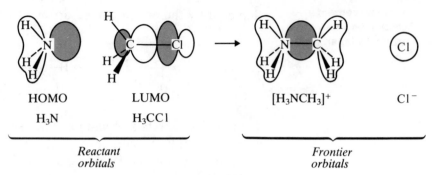

HOMO   LUMO $[H_3NCH_3]^+$ Cl^-

H_3N H_3CCl

Reactant   Frontier
orbitals   orbitals

Fig. 5.5 The interacting orbitals in the reaction of ammonia with chloroethane (not a scale drawing)

This was confirmed experimentally by studying the displacement of iodide anions from optically active secondary alkyl iodides, by radio-active iodide ions:

$$(+)RI + I^{*-} \rightleftharpoons (-)RI^* + I^-$$

The rate of exchange and the rate of inversion were identical:

The concept of a functional group is fundamental to the understanding of organic reactions, but at first sight the delocalized nature of the majority of the electrons in a polyatomic molecule appears to contradict this concept. In fact the frontier orbitals are usually arranged in a way which emphasizes the significance of the functional group. Thus the HOMO of methylamine (Fig. 5.6) has an energy and a shape very similar to ammonia. Similarly the LUMO of fluoroethane has a shape and an energy very similar to the LUMO of fluoromethane (Fig. 5.7).

It follows from the orbital pictures we have drawn that the overlap between the HOMO of one reagent with the LUMO of the other will be greatly affected by bulky adjacent groups (Fig. 5.8).

It is equally possible for the HOMO-gen to contain very bulky groups adjacent to the reaction site. Thus quinuclidine reacts 700 times faster with 2-iodo-2-methylpropane (t-butyl iodide) than triethylamine in which the freely rotating ethyl groups hinder the approach of the nitrogen lone pair (Fig. 5.9).

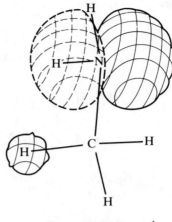

$$E = -230 \text{ kcal mol}^{-1}$$

Fig. 5.6   HOMO of methylamine

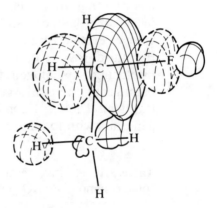

Fig. 5.7   LUMO of fluoroethane

$$
\begin{array}{ll}
\text{CH}_3- & 1 \\
\text{CH}_3\text{CH}_2- & 0.03 \\
(\text{CH}_3)_3\text{C}- & 0
\end{array}
$$

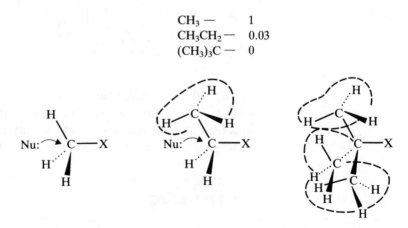

Fig. 5.8   Displacement reactions with increasingly substituted reaction centre

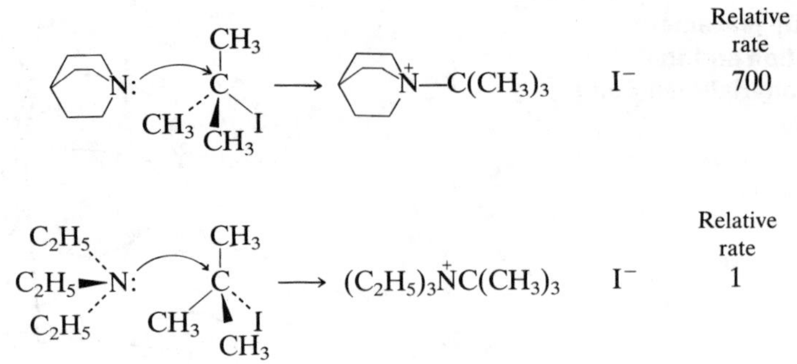

Fig. 5.9

In general there is a rough correlation between the basicity of a HOMO-gen and its reactivity in a concerted displacement reaction. Within one row of the periodic table it is generally true, so that ammonia is more effective in displacing a halogen in an alkyl halide than water. When we consider HOMO-gens whose reactive centre involves atoms from either the second or the third row (softer) they are invariably more effective in displacing, say halogen, than HOMO-gens whose reactive centre belongs to the same group but with a lower atomic number (harder). Table 5.1 compares the relative reactivity of HOMO-gen pairs with iodomethane.

Table 5.1 Relative reactivity in concerted displacement reactions of some common HOMO-gens

SOFT		*HARD*
	$HS^- > HO^-$	
	$Cl^- > F^-$	
	$C_6H_5S^- > C_6H_5O^-$	
	$(CH_3)_2S > (CH_3)_2O$	
	$(C_2H_5)_3P > (C_2H_5)_3N$	

The displacement reaction is probably the commonest reaction in organic chemistry. The important features of bimolecular kinetics, inversion at the reaction centre and the effect of substituents, are all well accounted for by pictorial orbital theory.

Further reading

Chemical Reactivity and Reaction Paths, ed. by G. Klopman, Wiley, Chichester, 1974.

Problems

1 Distinguish between 'charge control' and 'orbital control' and define which type of species are 'hard' and which are 'soft'.

2 Sketch the interacting orbitals when ethoxide anions displace chloride ions from chloroethane. Do not worry about the relative 'sign' of the chlorine orbitals, but be sure of the size of each lobe.

3 Thiolate anions (RS^-) are about 10^3 times as reactive in displacing a halogen from carbon as alkanolate anions (RO^-). Discuss the reasons for this.

4 Comment on the relative rates of replacement of chloride by iodide ion in acetone in the following series of compounds

Cl—O—OEt	Cl—≡N	Cl—O	Cl—O—C$_6$H$_5$
$k/k_{C_3H_7Cl}$ 1600	2800	3300	100,000

6 Bimolecular Elimination Reactions

We have seen that in orbital controlled displacement reactions the highest occupied molecular orbital of an electron donor (the HOMO-gen) interacts with the lowest unoccupied molecular orbital of an acceptor (the LUMO-gen) (see page 40). The essential requirements are (1) that the energies of the interacting orbitals are similar and (2) that the steric situation permits extensive overlap of the interacting orbitals. When the energies of the interacting orbitals are far apart a reaction can still occur if the polar situation is sufficiently favourable. This is the situation in many elimination reactions. The reaction still involves the interaction of the highest molecular orbital of a donor (e.g. CH_3O^-) and the lowest molecular orbital of an acceptor (e.g. CH_3CH_2F) (Fig. 6.1). However, the site of interaction in the acceptor molecule is governed by polarity, rather than by the maximum possible overlap of the frontier orbitals (Fig. 6.2).

The orbital electronegativity of a saturated carbon atom is less (i.e. softer) than that of the proton (which is harder). In the absence of dominant steric effects a soft HOMO-gen (a good electron donor) will favour attack on carbon and a displacement reaction will ensue; whereas a hard HOMO-gen will react with the proton and an elimination reaction will ensue. In solution there

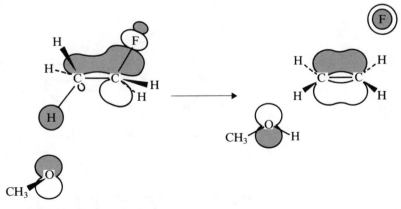

Fig. 6.1 Charge control

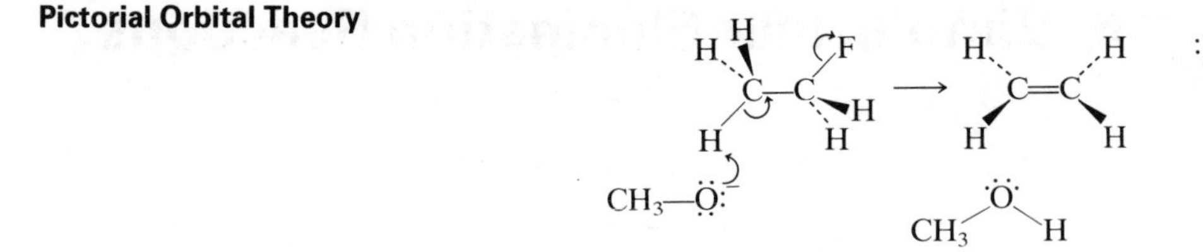

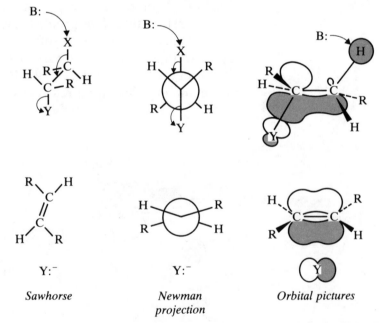

Fig. 6.2 The elimination reaction

is a further factor; the elimination reaction involves the removal of electrons from the donor with concurrent loss of solvation energy. The smaller the ionic radius of the atom from which the electrons are drawn the larger the solvation energy and the lower the energy of the orbital will be. In other words, charge controlled reactions involve species of high electronegativity and small ionic radii (high orbital electronegativity), e.g. NH_2^-, CH_3O^-. In contrast displacement reactions require weakly solvated donors which have high-lying occupied orbitals, relatively low electronegativity and large ionic radius (e.g. I^-, RS^-).

Bimolecular elimination of the kind we are discussing has fairly strict steric requirements. The two departing groups ('X' and 'Y') must be approximately anti-periplanar to each other. This is best seen in sawhorse or Newman projection formulae (Fig. 6.3). This requirement is derived from the spatial character-

Sawhorse   *Newman projection*   *Orbital pictures*

Fig. 6.3 Sawhorse and Newman projection formulae—illustrating steric pathway of concerted elimination reactions

istics of the LUMO of the acceptor molecule. The HOMO-gen approaches the LUMO-gen anti-periplanar to the leaving group and the reaction is normally completely stereospecific. For example the two possible 4-t-butyl-cyclohexyltrimethylammonium salts react differently with t-butoxy anions. The 4-t-butyl group freezes the molecules in the conformations shown in Fig. 6.4, (i.e. the t-butyl group must be equatorial) and the molecule with a hydrogen anti-periplanar to the quaternary ammonium group undergoes facile elimination. In the other isomer the equatorial quaternary ammonium group is approximately synclinal to the ring hydrogens and displacement on the quaternary nitrogen atom occurs instead.

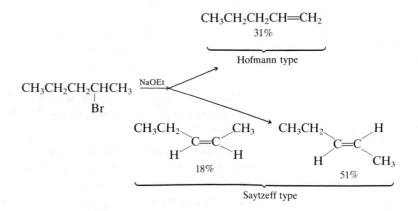

Fig. 6.4

When 2-bromopentane is heated with sodium ethoxide three elimination products are formed. The hydrogen is abstracted

preferentially from the most crowded site, and the preferred olefin is the one in which steric compression is a minimum (i.e. the *trans*-pentene-2 is favoured over the *cis*-pentene-2). Confirmation that steric effects play a major part in controlling the orientation comes from:

(a) changing the 'size' of the leaving group

$$CH_3CH_2CH_2\overset{\overset{\displaystyle X}{|}}{C}HCH_3 \longrightarrow \overset{A}{[CH_3CH_2CH_2CH=CH_2]} : \overset{B}{[CH_3CH_2CH=CHCH_3]}$$

	A/B	trans and cis
X = Br	0.45	
= $\overset{+}{S}(CH_3)_2$	6.7	
= $\overset{+}{N}(CH_3)_3$	50	

(b) increasing the extent of branching of the starting molecule

$$C_2H_5\overset{\overset{\displaystyle CH_3}{|}}{\underset{\underset{\displaystyle CH_3}{|}}{C}}Br \longrightarrow \left[\overset{A}{\underset{CH_3}{\overset{C_2H_5}{\diagdown}}C{=}CH_2}\right] : \left[\overset{B}{CH_3CH{=}C\overset{CH_3}{\diagup}_{\diagdown CH_3}}\right] \quad \begin{array}{c} A/B \\ 0.45 \end{array}$$

$$CH_3CH_2CH_2\overset{\overset{\displaystyle CH_3}{|}}{\underset{\underset{\displaystyle CH_3}{|}}{C}}Br \longrightarrow \left[\underset{CH_3}{\overset{C_3H_7}{\diagdown}}C{=}CH_2\right] : \left[C_2H_5CH{=}C\overset{CH_3}{\diagup}_{\diagdown CH_3}\right] \quad 1.0$$

$$CH_3\overset{\overset{\displaystyle CH_3}{|}}{\underset{\underset{\displaystyle CH_3}{|}}{C}}{-}CH_2{-}\overset{\overset{\displaystyle CH_3}{|}}{\underset{\underset{\displaystyle CH_3}{|}}{C}}Br \longrightarrow \left[\underset{CH_3}{\overset{(CH_3)_3C}{\diagdown}}C{=}CH_2\right] : \left[(CH_3)_3CCH{=}C\overset{CH_3}{\diagup}_{\diagdown CH_3}\right] \quad 6.1$$

(c) increasing the bulk of the attacking base B⁻

$$\underset{CH_3}{\overset{CH_3}{\diagdown}}CH{-}\overset{\overset{\displaystyle CH_3}{|}}{\underset{\underset{\displaystyle CH_3}{|}}{C}}{-}Br \xrightarrow{B^-} \left[\overset{X}{H{-}\overset{\overset{\displaystyle CH_3}{|}}{\underset{\underset{\displaystyle CH_3}{|}}{C}}{-}C\overset{CH_2}{\diagup}_{\diagdown CH_3}}\right] : \left[\overset{Y}{\underset{CH_3}{\overset{CH_3}{\diagdown}}C{=}C\overset{CH_3}{\diagup}_{\diagdown CH_3}}\right]$$

	X/Y
B⁻ = $C_2H_5O^-$	0.25
$(CH_3)_3CO^-$	2.7
$(C_2H_5)_3CO^-$	11.4

There are other reactions which lead to elimination but they are mechanistically different and will be discussed in later chapters.

The balance between displacement and elimination can be very fine, and very frequently both processes occur simultaneously. In general, raising the reaction temperature increases the proportion of elimination, i.e. the activation energy for elimination is greater than that for substitution. In contrast, elimination results in an increase in the number of particles so that the pre-exponential terms for elimination may be larger. In pictorial orbital terms, a soft HOMO-gen will favour displacement while a hard HOMO-gen will favour elimination.

Further reading

Elimination Reactions, D. U. Banthorpe, Elsevier, Amsterdam,
   1963.
Chemical Reactions and Reaction Paths, ed. by G. Klopman,
   Wiley, New York, 1976.

Problems

1 Contrast the requirements for displacement reactions with
   those for elimination reactions. Associate 'hard' and 'soft'
   reagents with particular reaction pathways.

2 Account for the change from displacement to elimination in
   the following bimolecular reactions of alkyl bromides. The
   reactions involve treatment with $NaOC_2H_5$ in ethanol at
   $55°C$.

	C_2H_5Br	$(CH_3)_2CHBr$	$(CH_3)_3CBr$
Displacement $10^5 k_d$	118.2	2.1	—
Elimination $10^5 k_e$	1.2	7.6	50
% Olefin	1.0	79	100

$$k_d \text{ and } k_e \text{ in } s^{-1}\,mol^{-1}\,l$$

3 Explain why the proportion of t-alkene increased as the
   pyridine became more substituted, when these two alkyl
   bromides were treated with the four substituted pyridines.

	$(CH_3)_2CH{-}\overset{\displaystyle Br}{C}(CH_3)_2$	$CH_3CH_2\overset{\displaystyle Br}{C}(CH_3)_2$
C_5H_5N	10	25
$4CH_3C_5H_4N$	—	25
$2CH_3C_5H_4N$	18	30
$2,6(CH_3)_2C_5H_3N$	38	45

4 In the reaction of 2-bromophenylethane with NaOEt in the
   presence of EtOD there is no deuterium incorporated in the
   unreacted bromide nor in the phenylethene produced. How
   does this fact relate to the mechanism of the reaction?

5 When treated with potassium hydroxide in ethanol, men-
   thylchloride (1) gives exclusively 2-menthene (2). Explain.

(1)   (2)

7 Addition Reactions

The energy required to break a carbon–carbon single bond is about $83.6\,\text{kcal mol}^{-1}$, but the energy required to uncouple one of the pairs of electrons in a 'double bond' only requires about $65\,\text{kcal mol}^{-1}$.

$$-\overset{|}{\underset{|}{C}}-\overset{|}{\underset{|}{C}}- \longrightarrow 2-\overset{|}{\underset{|}{C}}\cdot \qquad \Delta H \simeq +83.6\,\text{kcal mol}^{-1}$$

$$\overset{\diagdown}{\diagup}C{=}C\overset{\diagup}{\diagdown} \longrightarrow \overset{\diagdown}{\diagup}\dot{C}{-}\dot{C}\overset{\diagup}{\diagdown} \qquad \Delta H \simeq +65\quad \text{kcal mol}^{-1}$$

It follows that 'addition reactions' in which one such pair of electrons is uncoupled and two new 'single bonds' are formed will be exothermic.

$$CH_2{=}CH_2 + H_2 \longrightarrow CH_3CH_3 \qquad \Delta H \simeq -30\,\text{kcal mol}^{-1}$$

From a mechanistic point of view three types of a reaction can occur:

(a) Cationic addition

$$R^+ + \overset{\diagdown}{\diagup}C{=}C\overset{\diagup}{\diagdown} \xrightarrow[\text{slow}]{} R{-}\overset{|}{\underset{|}{C}}{-}\overset{|}{\underset{|}{C}}{^+} \xrightarrow[\text{fast}]{X^-} R{-}\overset{|}{\underset{|}{C}}{-}\overset{|}{\underset{|}{C}}{-}X$$

(b) Radical addition

$$R\cdot + \overset{\diagdown}{\diagup}C{=}C\overset{\diagup}{\diagdown} \longrightarrow R{-}\overset{|}{\underset{|}{C}}{-}\overset{|}{\underset{|}{C}}\cdot \xrightarrow{R-X} R{-}\overset{|}{\underset{|}{C}}{-}\overset{|}{\underset{|}{C}}{-}X\ (+R\cdot)$$

(c) Anionic addition

$$R{:}^- + \overset{\diagdown}{\diagup}C{=}C\overset{\diagup}{\diagdown} \longrightarrow R{-}\overset{|}{\underset{|}{C}}{-}\overset{|}{\underset{|}{C}}{:}^- \xrightarrow[\text{fast}]{X^+} R{-}\overset{|}{\underset{|}{C}}{-}\overset{|}{\underset{|}{C}}{-}X$$

Cationic and free radical addition are common with hydrocarbon olefins and their derivatives, but anionic addition will only occur when the olefinic double bond is flanked by 'electron attracting' or 'electron accepting' groups. Carbonyl and similar double bonds containing hetero-atoms react with both cationic and anionic reagents, though the orientation will differ. In simple cationic addition the orientation of the addition is determined by the interaction between the HOMO of the olefin and the LUMO of the attacking species (i.e. the reaction is orbital controlled).

(a) Cationic addition

The approach of a cation (i.e. the LUMO-gen) to an alkene will be such as to give maximum overlap with the HOMO of the olefin. The approach is therefore at right-angles to the molecular plane of the olefin. If the LUMO is small and dense, i.e. hard (e.g. a proton or a carbocation), maximum overlap will be obtained when the principal interaction occurs at one of the sp^2-carbon atoms, whereas when the LUMO is large and diffuse, i.e. soft (e.g. a bromonium ion, Br^+), maximum overlap will occur when the approach is at the centre of the π-orbital (the HOMO).* See Fig. 7.1. The initial adducts (a) and (b) rapidly

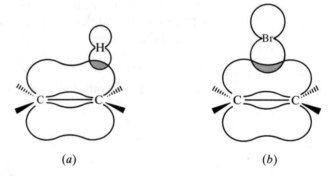

(a)   (b)

Fig. 7.1 The frontier orbital interaction between the HOMO of an olefin and (a) a small intense LUMO (e.g. H^+ or RCH_2^+) or (b) a large diffuse LUMO (e.g. Br^+)

undergo the second stage of the addition process (i.e. the interaction of the LUMO of the adduct cation with a HOMO-gen), but they will have different stereo-chemical pathways. The addition of a HOMO-gen which is small and in which the 'electron density' is concentrated (e.g. (a)) yields a new carbocation which has 'free' rotation in the adduct. If, in an olefin $R_1R_2C{=}CR_3R_4$, R_1 and R_2 are different and likewise R_3 and R_4 are different, the addition products will consist of two dl pairs (Fig. 7.2).

---

* N.m.r. clearly shows that the addition of a proton to propene yields the 2-propyl cation. There is however kinetic evidence that the addition of a proton involves the transient bridged structure (as for Br^+).

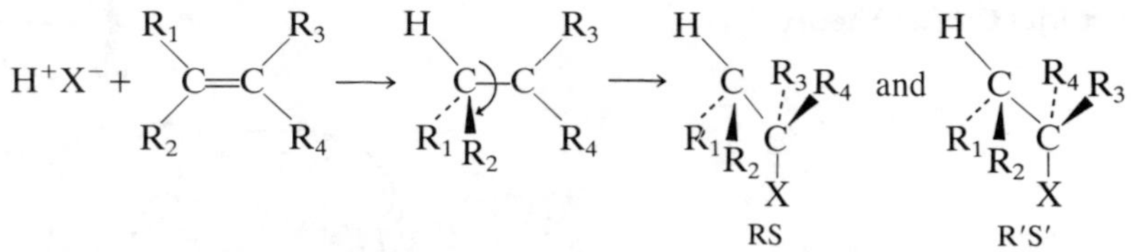

Fig. 7.2 Stereochemical consequences of addition of HX to an unsymmetric olefin

In contrast the addition of a bromonium ion leads to the formation of the bridged ion (e.g. (b)), and the incoming anion (a HOMO-gen) must approach anti-periplanar to the bridging bromine atom.

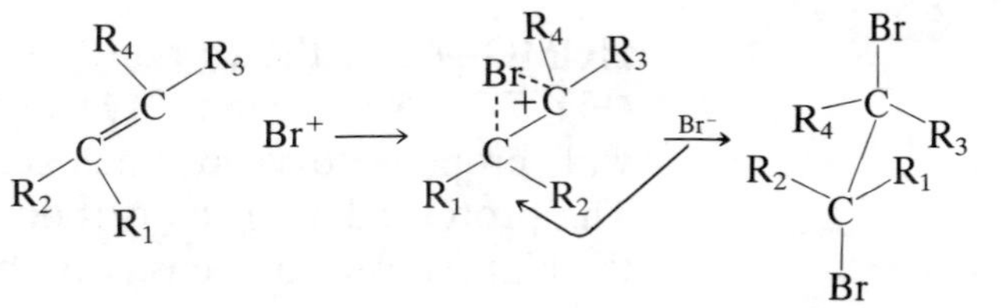

The stereochemistry can best be depicted by using the Newman projection formula

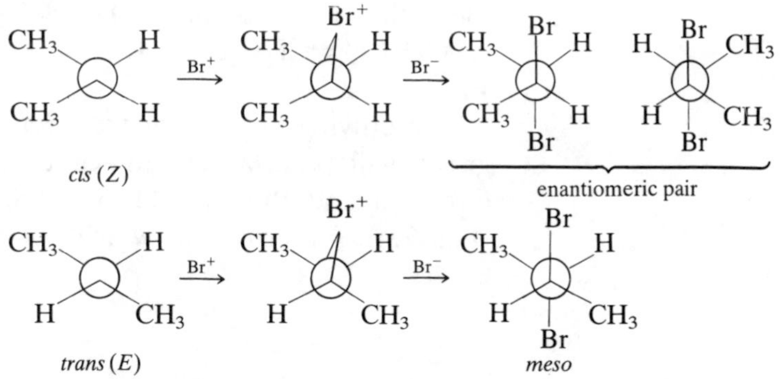

Although the addition of a hard reagent (e.g. a proton) to an olefin is not stereospecific it can be site specific if the olefin is unsymmetric. There are two factors which govern the orientation of a hard cation to an unsymmetric double bond: electronic effects and, to a much smaller extent, steric effects. An alkyl group is weakly electron repelling, so that the electron density in an adjacent double bond is not uniform. This small inequality is apparent in the HOMO of propene where it is possible to detect a slight shift of electron density away from the methyl-end of the double bond. Thus the LUMO of a hard reagent overlaps the

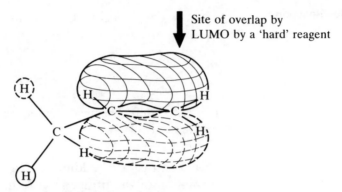

Site of overlap by
LUMO by a 'hard' reagent

Fig. 7.3 The HOMO of propene showing the slight shift of electron density away from the methyl group

HOMO-gen at the carbon remote from the methyl substituent (Fig. 7.3). A halogen acid HX (X = F, Cl or Br) therefore reacts with propene to yield 2-halogenopropane as the final product. The proton adds to the carbon atom of the propene which has the highest electron density in the HOMO. The methyl group by

$$H^+ + CH_3CH{=}CH_2 \longrightarrow CH_3\overset{+}{C}HCH_3 \longrightarrow CH_3CHXCH_3$$

releasing electrons facilitates the addition of suitable LUMO-gens; e.g. in the addition of bromonium ions to olefins the relative rates are $CH_2{=}CH_2$ 1.0; $C_2H_5CH{=}CH_2$ 97; *cis*-$CH_3CH{=}CHC_2H_5$ 4×10^8; $(CH_3)_2C{=}C(CH_3)_2$ 9.3×10^5.

A methyl group is electron repelling, but a trifluoromethyl group will polarize an adjacent double bond in the opposite direction and the orientation of cationic addition is reversed (Fig. 7.4). Other groups which polarize the π-orbitals of alkenes

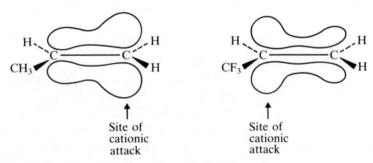

Site of
cationic
attack

Site of
cationic
attack

Fig. 7.4 Diagrams representing the polarization of bonding π-orbitals of propene and 3,3,3-trifluoropropene

$$CH_3CH{=}CH_2 + H^+ \longrightarrow CH_3\overset{+}{C}HCH_3 \longrightarrow CH_3CHXCH_3$$
$$CF_3CH{=}CH_2 + H^+ \longrightarrow CF_3CH_2\overset{+}{C}H_2 \longrightarrow CF_3CH_2CH_2X$$

so that the addition of a LUMO-gen occurs at the site of substitution include electron attracting groups like CCl_3— and the quaternary ammonium group. Esters of acrylic acid and

$$CH_2{=}CH\overset{+}{N}(CH_3)_3 \xrightarrow{\text{HCl}} ClCH_2CH_2\overset{+}{N}(CH_3)_3$$

other α,β-unsaturated carbonyl compounds also undergo addition to yield products in which the HOMO-gen adds to the β-position. Reactions of this type will be discussed below.

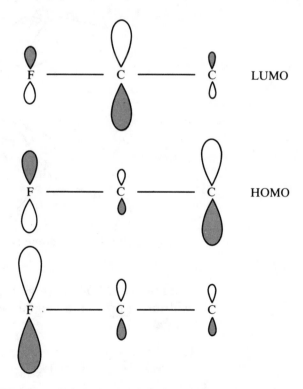

When the olefin carries an adjacent substituent with electrons in orbitals of π–symmetry the orientation is governed by the interaction of the orbitals of the substituent with the π-orbitals of the double bond. Thus we can depict the π-orbitals of vinyl fluoride (fluoroethene) as shown in Fig. 7.5. A LUMO-gen will attack the 'allyl-type' structure at the β-carbon atom, i.e. orbital control will lead to the new bond forming at the terminal

Fig. 7.5 Frontier orbitals of vinyl fluoride (illustrating symmetry and relative electron density but *not* representing true shape)

CH_2-group. In resonance theory this reaction would be depicted as follows:

$$X^+ + CH_2{=}CH{-}F \longrightarrow [XCH_2{-}\overset{+}{C}H{-}\ddot{F}\!: \longleftrightarrow XCH_2{-}CH{=}\overset{+}{\ddot{F}}\!:]$$

This latter argument is weak because it depends on the electronic situation at the end of a reaction in which the transition state is likely to be early (i.e. the transition state resembles the reactants).

The addition to the carbonyl double bond will mainly be dealt with below (under 'anionic addition') but a brief mention of acid catalyzed additions must be included here. The carbonyl double bond is much more polar than the substituted olefins we have discussed above, and more important the HOMO is a non-bonding orbital with most of the electron density centred on the oxygen atom.

A hard LUMO-gen like H^+ will therefore attack acetone (Fig. 7.6) at the oxygen atom leaving a positive charge concentrated on the carbonyl carbon atom. This will in turn react with a

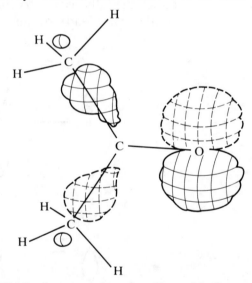

Fig. 7.6 HOMO of acetone (non-bonding orbital)

suitable HOMO-gen (e.g. methanol) and the resulting cation will lose a proton to yield a hemiketal (which can react further):

Cationic addition to acetone to yield a hemiketal

If there are two 'double bonds' separated by a 'single bond' (i.e. two conjugated double bonds) the frontier orbitals will extend over the four carbon atoms (cf. orbitals of butadiene, see Chapter 2, page 22). A species with a low lying anti-bonding orbital (LUMO-gen), e.g. H^+, will attack butadiene at a terminal position. The methyl substituted allyl cation so formed is now the LUMO-gen in the next step of the overall reaction and it will react in turn with a species containing a high energy HOMO (e.g. Cl^-) at two possible sites:

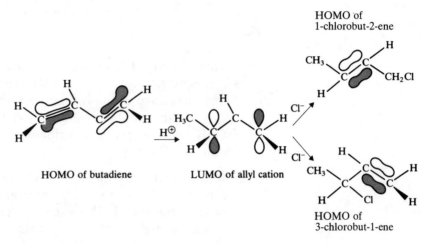

HOMO of butadiene   LUMO of allyl cation

HOMO of 1-chlorobut-2-ene

HOMO of 3-chlorobut-1-ene

Fig. 7.7 The addition of hydrogen chloride to 1,3-butadiene (frontier orbitals)

$$CH_2{=}CH{-}CH{=}CH_2 \xrightarrow{\;H^+\;} \begin{cases} CH_3CH{=}CH{-}\overset{+}{C}H_2 & CH_3CH{=}CHCH_2Cl \\[2mm] \updownarrow & \\[2mm] CH_3\overset{+}{C}HCH{=}CH_2 & CH_3CHClCH{=}CH_2 \end{cases}$$

The addition of hydrogen chloride to 1,3-butadiene (classical structures)

When one of the atoms in a 'conjugated double bond' is a hetero atom like oxygen as in acrolein [$CH_2{=}CH{-}CH{=}O$] the HOMO is a non-bonding orbital (cf. acetone above). The final HOMO-gen (Cl^-) will add to the terminal carbon atom, as in the butadiene example, to yield an *enol* which will rearrange to the keto form (Fig. 7.8).

We can summarize the factors which control cationic addition to olefins as follows:

(1) The reaction initially involves the interaction of the HOMO of the olefin with a LUMO-gen which is usually positively charged.

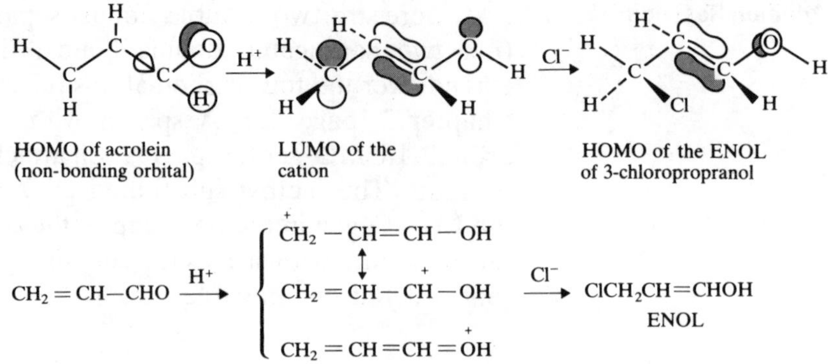

HOMO of acrolein
(non-bonding orbital)

LUMO of the
cation

HOMO of the ENOL
of 3-chloropropranol

$$CH_2=CH-CHO \xrightarrow{H^+} \begin{cases} \overset{+}{C}H_2-CH=CH-OH \\ \updownarrow \\ CH_2=\overset{}{C}H-\overset{+}{C}H-OH \\ CH_2=CH=CH=\overset{+}{O}H \end{cases} \xrightarrow{Cl^-} ClCH_2CH=CHOH$$

ENOL

Fig. 7.8

(2) If the adding LUMO-gen is hard the reaction is not stereo-specific, but if the LUMO-gen is diffuse (soft) then the second stage of the reaction is stereo-specific, the adduct 'bridging' the double bond so that the final addition of a HOMO-gen occurs anti-periplanar to the addition of the initial LUMO-gen.

(3) The regiospecificity of the reaction depends on polarity and electron delocalization. The reaction is orbital controlled and the attacking LUMO-gen is electron deficient so that the site of highest electron density in the HOMO of the olefin interacts with the site of highest potential electron density in the LUMO of the attacking species.

(b) Radical addition

In the addition of a cation to an olefin, the frontier orbital interaction is between the LUMO of the cation and the HOMO of the olefin, and within the frontier orbital approximation only two electrons are involved. In the addition of a radical to an olefin two interactions involving frontier orbitals are possible. Either the SOMO of the radical takes the role of a LUMO and interacts with the HOMO of the olefin and three electrons are involved, or the SOMO of the radical takes the role of a HOMO and interacts with the LUMO of the olefin and only one electron is involved. Radical addition is less exothermic and the transition state later than with cationic addition, i.e. the transition state more resembles the products. Radicals are not ionic species (we are not at present considering radical ions), but as Fig. 7.9 suggests radical addition reactions are affected by the relative energies of the SOMO and the HOMO. Steric effects, which are only of minor importance in the addition reactions of

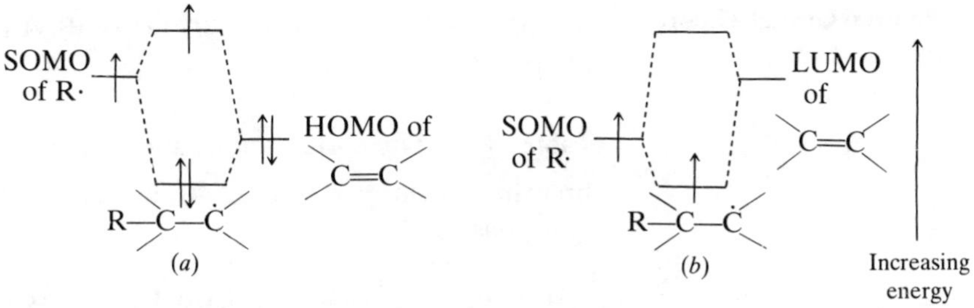

Fig. 7.9 Relative energy levels of the radical R·, the olefin $>C=C<$ and adduct radical R—C̈—Ċ (a) the radical R· as a LUMO-gen and (b) radical R· as a HOMO-gen. (a) and (b) should not be compared with each other, i.e the energy R—C—C· for (a) is not the same as the energy for (b)).

cations, are of major importance in determining the orientation of radical addition to unsymmetric olefins.

We can compare the reactivity of radicals by considering the reactions of methyl and trifluoromethyl radicals. The methyl radical is relatively electron repelling whereas the trifluoromethyl radical is electron attracting. In terms of the above diagram the methyl radical exhibits the characteristic properties of a HOMO-gen while the trifluoromethyl radical exhibits the characteristic properties of a LUMO-gen. The resultant polarity is illustrated by comparing the rates of addition of methyl and the fluoromethyl radicals to ethene and tetrafluoroethene. Table 7.1 shows a variation of relative rate of two orders of magnitude. However, steric effects can also

Table 7.1 The ratio of the addition of methyl and fluoromethyl radicals to ethene and tetrafluoroethene

Radical $k_{C_2F_4}^{164°}/k_{C_2H_4}^{164°}$	$CH_3·$	$CH_2F·$	$CHF_2·$	$CF_3·$
	9.5	3.4	1.1	0.1

be of considerable importance. Thus trifluoromethyl radicals add preferentially to *both* propene and 3,3,3-trifluoropropene at the CH_2— end of the double bond in sharp contrast to the addition of cations to the same olefins described above (Table 7.2). The importance of steric effects is illustrated by the

Table 7.2 Orientation ratios for the addition of $CF_3·$ to propene and 3,3,3-trifluoropropene

α β $CH_2=CHCH_3$	α β	α β $CH_2=CHCF_3$	α β
	1:0.09		1:0.02

orientation of branched perfluoro-alkyl radicals to vinyl fluoride (Table 7.3).

Table 7.3 The orientation and relative rate of the addition of branched-chain perfluoroalkyl radicals to vinyl fluoride $\overset{\alpha}{C}H_2{=}\overset{\beta}{C}HF$ (gas phase 164°)

Radical	$CF_3\cdot$	$CF_3CF_2\cdot$	$(CF_3)_2CF\cdot$	$(CF_3)_3C\cdot$
$\alpha:\beta$	1:0.1	1:0.06	1:0.02	1:0.005
$2k_\alpha/k_c$	0.5	0.5	0.5	0.5

k_c = rate constant for addition to $CH_2{=}CH_2$

Steric effects govern the orientation of addition of radicals to olefins, while polarity affects both orientation and relative rate. The effects can be in opposition and in a few cases the preferred orientation to a particular olefin is reversed when the attacking radical changes from methyl to trifluoromethyl. The Reactivity Selectivity Principle which implies a decrease in selectivity with increasing reactivity breaks down in these radical reactions. Thus:

$$
\begin{array}{lll}
32\% & CH_3CHF\dot{C}F_2 \\
68\% & \dot{C}HFCF_2CH_3
\end{array}
\Bigg\}
\xleftarrow[\;]{CH_3\cdot}
\underset{164°}{CHF{=}CF_2}
\xrightarrow{\;CF_3\cdot\;}
\Bigg\{
\begin{array}{ll}
CF_3CHF\dot{C}F_2 & 95\% \\
\dot{C}HFCF_2CF_3 & 5\%
\end{array}
$$

The $CF_3\cdot$ radical is both the more reactive and more selective, because as well as having the lower SOMO it leads to the more polar transition state.

(c) Anionic addition

Anions will not add to hydrocarbon olefins under normal reaction conditions, but if a double bond is adequately flanked by electron withdrawing groups addition may occur. Thus base-catalyzed addition of alcohols to polyfluoro-alkenes occurs quite readily:

$$(CF_3)_2C{=}CF_2 + CH_3OH \xrightarrow{Na^+OCH_3^-} (CF_3)_2CHCF_2OCH_3$$

The orientation is probably part determined by steric factors, but orbital interaction predominates. The HOMO of the methoxide ion would be expected to overlap with the olefin where the coefficient of its LUMO was a maximum and this will be at the terminal carbon atom.

The most important and common example of anionic addition is the addition of HOMO-gens to the LUMOs of a carbonyl bond. In the discussion of cationic addition (see above) we included acid-catalyzed addition to the carbonyl group, which involved the proton as LUMO-gen interacting with the HOMO of the carbonyl, followed by the addition of a further HOMO-gen to complete the reaction

$$\begin{array}{c}R\\\ \ \ \ C{=}O + H^+ \longrightarrow\\R\end{array} \quad \begin{array}{c}R\\\ \ \ \ \overset{+}{C}{-}OH \xrightarrow{CH_3OH}\\R\end{array} \quad \begin{array}{c}R\ \ \ OH\\\ \ \ \ C\\R\ \ \ OCH_3\end{array} + H^+$$

We are now considering the addition of a HOMO-gen, which involves interaction with the LUMO of the carbonyl compound (Fig. 7.10).

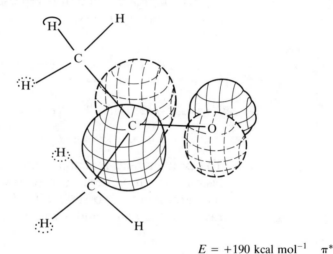

$E = +190 \text{ kcal mol}^{-1} \quad \pi^*$

Fig. 7.10　LUMO of acetone

Clearly maximum overlap between the HOMO of the donor will occur at the carbonyl carbon

$$\begin{array}{c}R\\\ \ \ \ C{=}O + CN^- \longrightarrow\\R\end{array} \quad \begin{array}{c}R\ \ \ O^-\\\ \ \ \ C \xrightarrow{H^+}\\R\ \ \ CN\end{array} \quad \begin{array}{c}R\ \ \ OH\\\ \ \ \ C\\R\ \ \ CN\end{array}$$

We have seen that if two 'classical' double bonds are separated by a single bond the frontier orbitals will extend over the four carbon atoms (see also the orbitals of butadiene, Chapter 2). In an exactly similar way the frontier orbitals of acrolein extend over the four conjugated atoms. In particular the LUMO of acrolein (π_3^*) has its greatest density at the 1- and 3- carbon atoms (Fig. 7.11).

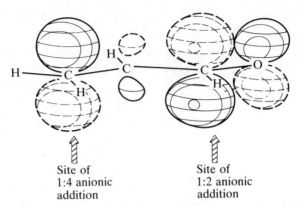

Site of
1:4 anionic
addition

Site of
1:2 anionic
addition

Fig. 7.11 The LUMO of acrolein and the sites of attack by the HOMO of a donor

This conjugate addition is represented by resonance theory in terms of curved arrows:

$$CH_2{=}CH{-}CH{=}O \xrightarrow{HX} CH_2{=}CH{-}CHOH$$

1,2-addition

$$X \cdot CH_2{=}CH{-}CH{=}O \xrightarrow{HX} [XCH_2{-}CH{=}CH{-}OH] \longrightarrow XCH_2CH_2CH{=}O$$

enol

1,4-addition

The predominant reaction is normally the 1,4-addition probably because the initial enol can rearrange to the aldehyde; no such rearrangement is possible with the 1,2-adduct which can easily revert to the anion and acrolein.

Conclusion

The main characteristic of double bonds in either olefins or carbonyl compounds is their ability to take part in addition reactions. Three types of linear addition occur (cyclo-addition will be discussed later) in which the attacking reagent is either a LUMO-gen (cationic), a SOMO-gen (radical) or a HOMO-gen (anionic). Pictorial orbital theory accounts for the orientation, relative rate and, where applicable, the stereo-chemistry of all three types of addition reaction.

Further reading

Electrophilic Addition to Unsaturated Systems, P. B. D. de la Mare and R. Bolton, Elsevier, Amsterdam, 1966.

Frontier Orbitals and Chemical Reactions, I. Fleming, Wiley, Chichester, 1976.

Problems

1 Draw the frontier orbitals of acetone and indicate how this molecule will react with an anion (e.g. OH^-) or a cation (e.g. H^+).

2 Explain why the addition of Br_2 to an olefin usually occurs in an anti-periplanar (i.e. *trans*) position while the addition of HBr is usually non stereo-specific.

3 Predict the orientation of the addition of HCl to $CH_2{=}CHCH_3$; $CH_2{=}CHF$; $CH_2{=}CHCF_3$ and $CH_2{=}CHCO_2C_2H_5$. Draw the appropriate frontal orbitals.

4 Predict the orientation of addition of trifluoromethyl radicals with propene ($CH_3CH{=}CH_2$) and 3,3,3-trifluoropropene ($CF_3CH{=}CH_2$).

5 Diethyl malonate adds to ethyl crotonate in the presence of sodium ethoxide:

$$(C_2H_5O_2C)_2CH_2 + CH_3CH{=}CHCO_2C_2H_5 \longrightarrow \begin{array}{l} CH_3CH{-}CH_2CO_2C_2H_5 \\ \quad | \\ CH(CO_2C_2H_5)_2 \end{array}$$

Draw the appropriate frontier orbital of ethyl crotonate.

8 Ambident Reagents

The enolate anion (I) will react with bromomethane to give the *C*-alkylated product, whereas with the triethyloxonium ion *O*-alkylation occurs

$$[RCH—CH—O]^-$$

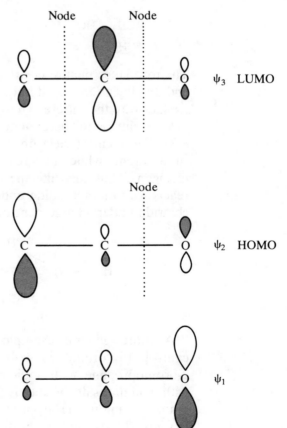

$$\underset{CH_3Br}{} \quad I \quad \underset{(C_2H_5)_3O^+}{}$$

$$\underset{|}{R}$$

$$CH_3CH—CHO \qquad RCH{=}CH—OC_2H_5$$

The three π_{CC} orbitals of the enolate anion are shown diagrammatically (Fig. 8.1). The diagrams represent the relative

Fig. 8.1

sign (by shading) and relative magnitude of the wave function (by size) at each atom, they are *not* intended to represent shape. These orbitals should be compared with those for allyl (page 19).

The charge density at any particular atom is the sum of the electron density of each of the occupied orbitals at that atom. In the enolate anion the charge density is greatest at the oxygen. A charge controlled process will therefore result in the new bond being formed at the oxygen. In contrast an orbital controlled process will involve bond formation at the terminal carbon where the coefficient of the HOMO is largest, shown as the biggest lobe in the diagram.

It is useful to compare the orbital picture with the resonance representation, which distinguishes between thermodynamic (orbital) and kinetic (charge) control.

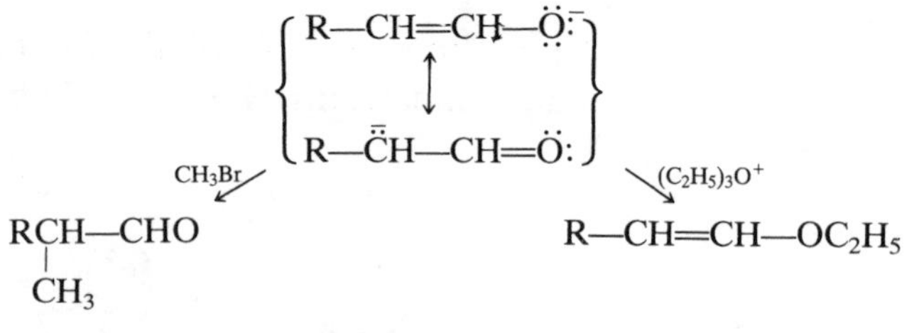

$$
\left\{
\begin{array}{c}
R\!-\!CH\!=\!CH\!-\!\ddot{\underset{\cdot\cdot}{O}}\!:^{-} \\[4pt]
\updownarrow \\[4pt]
R\!-\!\overset{-}{\underset{\cdot\cdot}{C}}H\!-\!CH\!=\!\ddot{O}\!:
\end{array}
\right\}
$$

$$CH_3Br \swarrow \qquad\qquad \searrow (C_2H_5)_3O^+$$

$$
\underset{\underset{\displaystyle CH_3}{|}}{RCH\!-\!CHO} \qquad\qquad\qquad R\!-\!CH\!=\!CH\!-\!OC_2H_5
$$

The resonance picture clearly provides a mechanism for both *C*- and *O*-alkylation but it requires further ad hoc arguments to explain why the different reagents produce different products.

Very similar to the enolate ion is the thiocyanate anion (Fig. 8.2). The greatest electron density in the HOMO (π_2) is on the sulfur atom, while the greatest total charge density is on the nitrogen. Thus just like the enolate anion the thiocyanate ion reacts with methyl iodide under 'orbital control' and with acetyl chloride under 'charge control'.

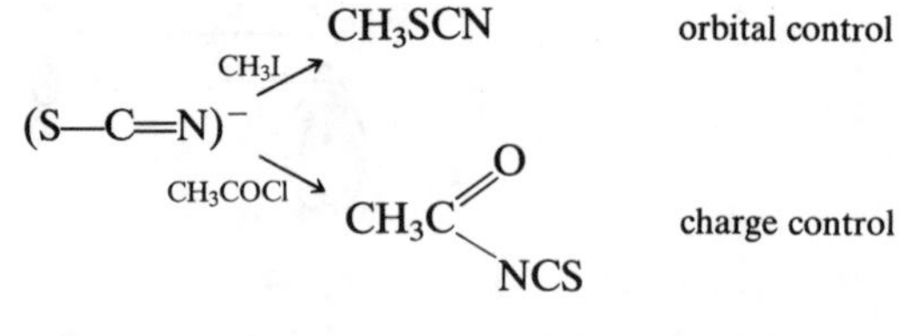

$$ \qquad\qquad\qquad CH_3SCN \qquad\qquad \text{orbital control}$$

$$(S\!-\!C\!\equiv\!N)^- \overset{CH_3I\;\nearrow}{\underset{CH_3COCl\;\searrow}{}}$$

$$ CH_3C\!\!\underset{NCS}{\overset{\displaystyle O}{\big<}} \qquad\qquad \text{charge control}$$

A more general example of the transition from 'charge control' to 'orbital control' is provided by the reactions of 2-bromopropane with sodium ethoxide on the one hand and with sodium salt of diethyl malonate on the other. In the ethoxide anion the negative charge is concentrated on the oxygen (hard) and it abstracts a proton (also hard) from 2-bromopropane to form a strong oxygen-hydrogen bond,

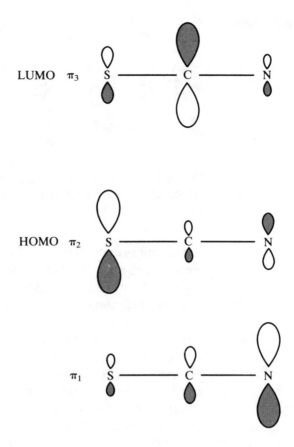

Fig. 8.2

concurrently with the expulsion of a bromide anion and the formation of π_{CC} orbitals between two of the carbon atoms. In contrast diethyl malonate ions, in which the negative charge is widely delocalized (soft), attack the carbon atom to which the bromine is attached, and a new carbon–carbon bond is formed with the concurrent displacement of a bromide anion.

$$
\begin{array}{c}
\text{CH}_2{=}\text{CHCH}_3 \quad \text{charge control} \\
\text{Elimination} \\
\overset{+-}{\text{NaOC}_2\text{H}_5} \nearrow \\
\begin{array}{c}\text{CH}_3\\ \diagdown\\ \text{CHBr}\\ \diagup\\ \text{CH}_3\end{array} \underset{\overset{+-}{\text{NaCH(CO}_2\text{C}_2\text{H}_5)_2}}{\searrow} \\
\begin{array}{c}\text{CH}_3\\ \diagdown\\ \text{CHCH(CO}_2\text{C}_2\text{H}_5)_2 \quad \text{orbital control}\\ \diagup\\ \text{CH}_3\end{array} \\
\text{Displacement}
\end{array}
$$

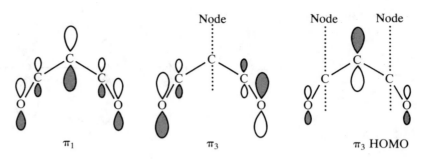

Fig. 8.3 Diagram representing π_{CC} orbitals of the malonate (or acetoacetate) anions (neglecting contributions from the n-orbitals of the alkyl oxygen ions)

The important difference between the two processes is that the reaction with the diethyl malonate ions involves two nearly degenerate orbitals (both centred on carbon), while the reaction with ethoxide ions involves orbitals of widely separated energies (one centred on carbon and one on oxygen). In the reaction with malonate ions the charge is dispersed while in the reaction with ethoxide the charge is concentrated. The orbital diagrams in Fig. 8.3 clearly show that for an orbital controlled process, attack will occur at the central carbon atom where the HOMO is a maximum, even though the charge density is highest on the two carbonyl oxygen atoms.

A very similar example is provided by the reaction of 1,2-dichloroethane with methoxide anions and thiol anions. Oxygen is more electronegative than either sulfur or carbon which both have very similar electronegativities. The sulfur-hydrogen bond in thiols (RS—H) is weaker than the oxygen-hydrogen bonds in alcohols (RO—H) and likewise the charge is more diffuse in the thiol anion than in the alkoxide anion. Thus orbital interaction of the thiol anion with the saturated carbon is a much more favourable process than similar interaction with the methoxide ion. In contrast the more electronegative oxygen abstracts a β-proton to form a strong oxygen-hydrogen bond.

$$\begin{array}{ccc}
& \text{CHCl}=\text{CH}_2 & \text{Elimination (charge control)} \\
\text{CH}_3\text{O}^- \nearrow & & \\
\text{CH}_2\text{Cl}-\text{CH}_2\text{Cl} & & \\
\text{C}_6\text{H}_5\text{S}^- \searrow & & \\
& \text{C}_6\text{H}_5\text{SCH}_2\text{CH}_2\text{SC}_6\text{H}_5 & \text{Displacement (orbital control)}
\end{array}$$

We saw that with bromopropane the malonate anion took part in an 'orbital controlled' displacement. If however the alkyl group is replaced by a more electronegative and more charge localized group 'charge control' may ensue. Thus the ethyl acetoacetate anion reacts with acetyl chloride to give the *O*-acylated product.

The *C*-alkylation involves interaction of two nearly degenerate carbon orbitals while the *O*-acylation involves a site bearing two electron attracting groups (carbonyl and chlorine). The ratio of *C*-alkylation to *O*-alkylation can be changed by alternating the leaving groups.

X =	I^-	Br^-	Ts^-	$EtSO_4^-$	$CF_3SO_3^-$
k_C/k_0	100	60	6.6	4.8	3.7

As X becomes more electronegative so the proportion of *O*-alkylation increases because charge is more concentrated, although *C*-alkylation predominates in all cases. It is important to appreciate that the change from orbital control usually involves a range of reactions where both types of process occur simultaneously.

Very similar data is available for $CH_3CH_2CH_2X$ (where X = Cl, Br, I).

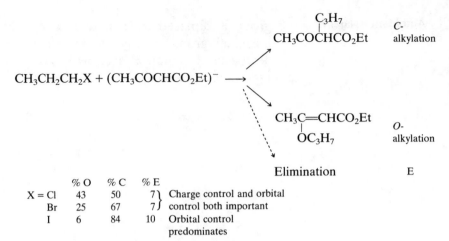

	% O	% C	% E	
X = Cl	43	50	7	Charge control and orbital
Br	25	67	7	control both important
I	6	84	10	Orbital control predominates

Another example of the same kind:

'O' *Charge control*   'C' *Orbital control*

	R = C$_6$H$_5$CH$_2$		R = p-O$_2$NC$_6$H$_4$CH$_2$
Cl	40% C	k_c^{Cl}	⎧ 90% C
	50% O		⎪ 2% O
Br	64% C	$k_c^{I}/k_c^{Cl} = 4500$	⎨ 66% C
	29% O		⎪ 24% O
I	70% C		⎪ 74% C
	15% O		⎩ 19% O

The change in the relative proportions of 'orbital control' and 'charge control' is also illustrated by the reaction of *para*-substituted phenoxide ions with 1-bromo-2-phenylethane.

$p\text{-RC}_6\text{H}_4\text{O}^- + \text{C}_6\text{H}_5\text{CH}_2\text{CH}_2\text{Br}$

$\xrightarrow{k_E}$ $p\text{-RC}_6\text{H}_4\text{OH} + \text{C}_6\text{H}_5\text{CH}=\text{CH}_2 + \text{Br}^-$ Charge control

$\xrightarrow{k_D}$ $p\text{-RC}_6\text{H}_4\text{OCH}_2\text{CH}_2\text{C}_6\text{H}_5 + \text{Br}^-$ Orbital control

R	CH$_3$O—	CH$_3$—	H—	Br—	CH$_3$CO—	O$_2$N—
k_E/k_D	0.94	0.93	0.86	0.52	0.30	0.20

Other ambient ions include imines:

$$CH_3-\overset{\overset{\displaystyle C_6H_5}{|}}{C}=N-C_6H_5 \longrightarrow CH_2{=}\overset{\overset{\displaystyle C_6H_5}{|}}{C}-\overset{..}{\underset{}{N}}-C_6H_5$$

$$CH_3CH_2-\overset{\overset{\displaystyle C_6H_5}{|}}{C}{=}NC_6H_5$$
Orbital

$$\overset{..}{\underset{}{C}}H_2-\overset{\overset{\displaystyle C_6H_5}{|}}{C}=N-C_6H_5 \xrightarrow{EtX}$$

$$CH_2{=}\overset{\overset{\displaystyle C_6H_5}{|}}{\underset{\underset{\displaystyle C_2H_5}{|}}{C}}-NC_6H_5$$
Charge

	EtX = EtI	EtX = Et$_2$SO$_4$	EtX = EtBF$_4^-$Et$_2$O
N/C	0.1	1.2	22

Orbital control $\longleftarrow$ $\longrightarrow$ Charge control $\longrightarrow$

The change from elimination to displacement cannot be explained in terms of resonance theory. In contrast, pictorial orbital theory shows the change in reaction pathway to be due to a change from 'charge control' to 'orbital control'.

Further reading

Alternative Proton Sites, M. Liles in *Advances in Physical Organic Chemistry*, Academic Press, New York, 1975.
Chemical Reactivity and Reaction Paths, ed. G. Klopman, Wiley, New York, 1974.

Problems

1 Account for the following ratios of products in terms of orbital versus charge control.

$$CH_3\overset{\overset{\displaystyle O}{||}}{C}{-}CHCO_2Et + RX$$

$$\overset{\overset{\displaystyle OR}{|}}{CH_3C}{=}CHCO_2Et \qquad CH_3\overset{\overset{\displaystyle O}{||}}{C}{-}CH_2CO_2Et \qquad \overset{\overset{\displaystyle OR}{|}}{CH_3C}{=}\overset{\overset{}{}}{\underset{\underset{\displaystyle R}{|}}{C}}CO_2Et \qquad CH_3CO\overset{\overset{\displaystyle R}{|}}{\underset{\underset{\displaystyle R}{|}}{C}}CO_2Et$$

	A	B	C	D
R = (CH$_3$)$_2$CHCl	81	19	0	0
X = n-C$_3$H$_7$Cl	61	23	8	8
= C$_2$H$_5$Br	46	34	16	14
= CH$_3$I	14	58	28	0

Products %

2 *p*-Toluene sulfonate anions are 'hard' compared with bromides and iodides which are 'soft'. Account for the observed rate constant ratio of the displacement reactions of alkyl tosylates and the corresponding alkyl bromides:

$$k_{Ts}/k_{Br}$$

$$C_2H_5X \xrightarrow{C_2H_5OH} C_2H_5OC_2H_5 \qquad 15$$

$$CH_3X \xrightarrow{C_2H_5O^-} CH_3OC_2H_5 \qquad 5$$

$$CH_3X \xrightarrow{RS^-} CH_3SR \qquad 0.3$$

$$n\text{-}C_4H_9X \xrightarrow{I^-} n\text{-}C_4H_9I \qquad 0.3$$

3 The halogens become 'softer' in the order Cl Br I. With this in mind account for the product composition in the alkylation of ethyl aceto-acetate.

$$CH_3COCH_2CO_2Et + n\text{-}C_4H_9X \xrightarrow[\text{(CH}_3)_2\text{NCHO}]{K_2CO_3\ 100^\circ} CH_3COCHCO_2Et \quad \text{and} \quad CH_3C=CHCO_2Et$$

$$\underset{\displaystyle C_4H_9}{\big|} \qquad\qquad \underset{\displaystyle OC_4H_9}{\big|}$$

X = Cl	54%	46%
= Br	67%	33%
= I	99%	1%

4 The alkyl groups become 'harder' when branched at the *α*-position. Account for the following product ratios in these terms.

$$\underset{\text{when } R = n\text{-}C_3H_7}{CH_3\overset{\displaystyle O^-}{\overset{\|}{C}}=CHCOCH_3} + RBr \longrightarrow CH_3CO\overset{\displaystyle R}{\underset{}{\big|}}CHCOCH_3 \quad \text{and} \quad CH_3\overset{\displaystyle OR}{\underset{}{\big|}}C=CHCOCH_3$$

when R = *n*-C$_3$H$_7$	97%	3%
R = (CH$_3$)$_2$CH	73%	27%

9 Reactive Intermediates

Trivalent carbon

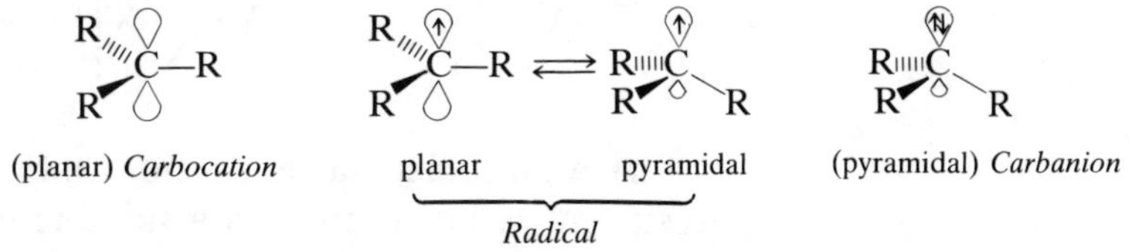

(planar) *Carbocation*   planar   pyramidal   (pyramidal) *Carbanion*

Radical

Fig. 9.1

Carbocations,* free radicals and carbanions (Fig. 9.1) are most frequently encountered as transient intermediates, although persistent examples of each exist. However this chapter is principally concerned with carbocations and carbanions as reactive intermediates.

Carbocations*

1-Phenyl-1-chloroethane is hydrolyzed to 1-phenylethanol at a rate that is independent of the hydroxide ion concentration. Similarly it is converted to the ethyl ether on treatment with ethanol and to phenylethyl acetate on treatment with acetic acid; in each case the rate of reaction is independent of the ethoxide or acetate anion concentration.

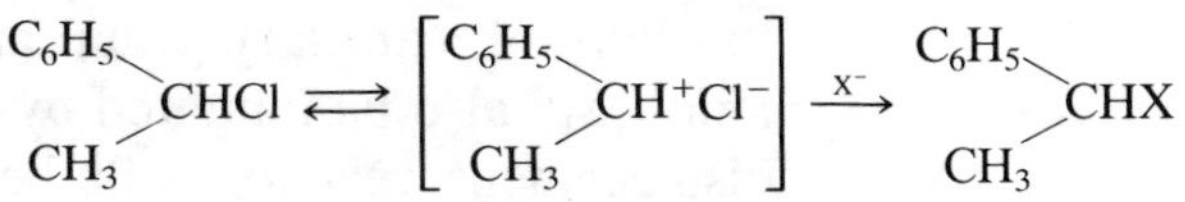

$$X = OH, OC_2H_5, OCOCH_3$$

Unimolecular substitution reaction

The simplest explanation is that the carbon–chlorine bond breaks spontaneously to yield a transient carbocation. Notice that this is in sharp contrast to the displacement reaction of alkyl

---

* Positively charged trivalent species (R_3C^+) are called 'carbocations' thus replacing the term 'carbonium ion'.

halides which involves a concerted process, and also involves a stereochemical inversion at the reaction site (see Chapter 5). If optically active 1-phenyl-1-chloroethane is hydrolyzed, the resulting 1-phenylethanol is racemized exactly as we would expect if the reaction proceeded via a planar carbocation.

There are thus two mechanisms by which a substitution in an aliphatic compound can take place:

(i) a bimolecular displacement

or

(ii) a unimolecular ionization, followed by the reaction of the resulting carbocation with a suitable electron pair donor

The bimolecular displacement involves an inversion, while the unimolecular process would be expected to be associated with racemization. In practice, there is usually some inversion because the departing anion inhibits the approach of the incoming anion (or electron donor) from that side of the molecule.

The unimolecular mechanism occurs in preference to the bimolecular process when the intermediate carbocation is stabilized by electron delocalization and/or by release of steric strain. Thus in reactions in which chlorine is replaced by hydroxide, primary alkyl halides react with the hydroxide anion by a concerted displacement, whereas tertiary alkyl halides react predominantly by the two-step ionization mechanism. The change in mechanism is associated with both polar and steric effects. The bimolecular displacement mechanism is retarded by the bulk of a tertiary group and the approach of the attacking anion will also be inhibited by electron repelling groups, i.e. the displacement reaction will be disfavoured in a tertiary alkyl halide. In contrast, the ionization mechanism will predominate when the charge is spread, i.e. the reaction site is branched; and if the reaction site is crowded then formation of a carbocation will help to release steric compression. In some cases the carbocation is resonance stabilized, e.g. the triphenylmethyl cation, in which circumstances the two-stage carbocation mechanism completely predominates.

The displacement reaction involves concerted inversion and the two-step ionization mechanism involves racemization (with some inversion). There is however a particular class of compounds which react with bases to yield products which result from the complete retention of configuration. The compounds in question are α-bromo-(or α-chloro-) carboxylic acids, e.g. RCHBrCO$_2$H, which under mild conditions hydrolyze to the corresponding 2-hydroxycarboxylic acids. The reaction is first order, i.e. independent of the concentration of the electron donor, hence the first step must be heterolysis to yield a bromide anion and a neutral intermediate. Two structures appear possible for this intermediate, and these are shown in Fig. 9.2. The trimethylene methane intermediate appears to be a

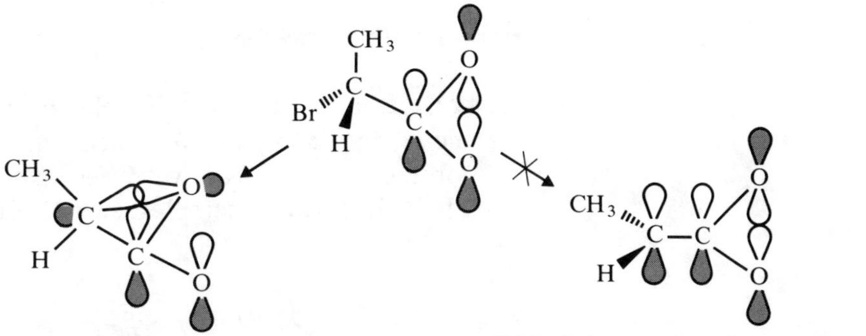

'Epoxy intermediate'   'Trimethylene methane intermediate'

Fig. 9.2

more delocalized structure but in fact there is only one bonding π-orbital in trimethylene methane whereas the epoxide has bonding σ- and π-molecular orbitals. More important the 'epoxide intermediate' requires any incoming anion to approach along the same pathway as the bromide anion departed, i.e. the reaction must proceed with complete retention of configuration.

An important characteristic of many carbocations is the ease with which they undergo rearrangement. The best known rearrangement is the pinacol–pinacolone reaction:

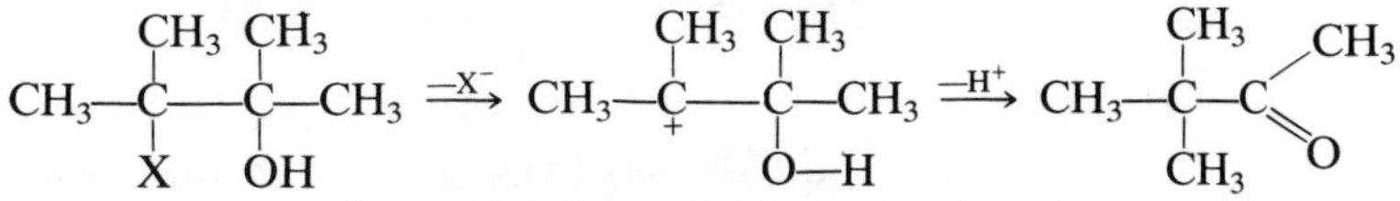

(Only orbitals involved in the reaction shown)

The reaction is a concerted process and examination of the orbital interaction (Fig. 9.3) confirms that the migrating group, if chiral, moves with retention of configuration.

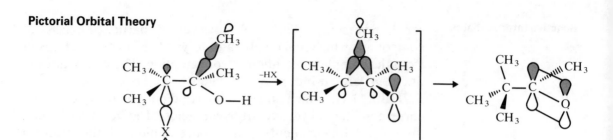

(Only orbitals involved directly in the reaction shown)

Fig. 9.3

Radicals (see Chapter 4)

Carbon radicals can exist as planar π-radicals or pyramidal σ-radicals; for example, even such simple radicals as methyl or trifluoromethyl radicals have different ground state geometries (Fig. 9.4). In certain examples, steric requirements of the radical

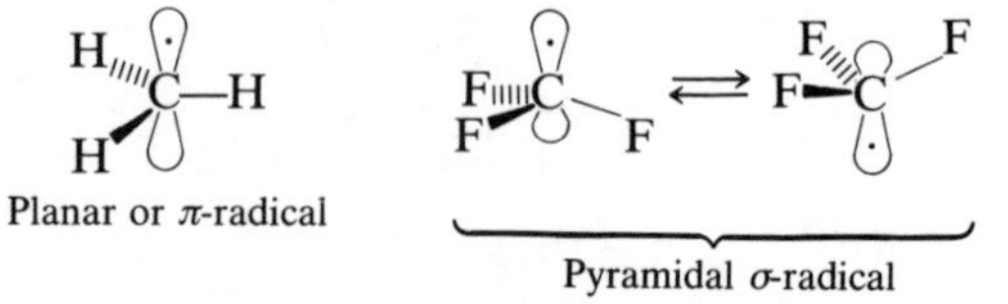

Planar or π-radical   Pyramidal σ-radical

Fig. 9.4

provide constraints which mean that interconversion from σ- to π-radical is difficult (Fig. 9.5). It has been suggested that certain

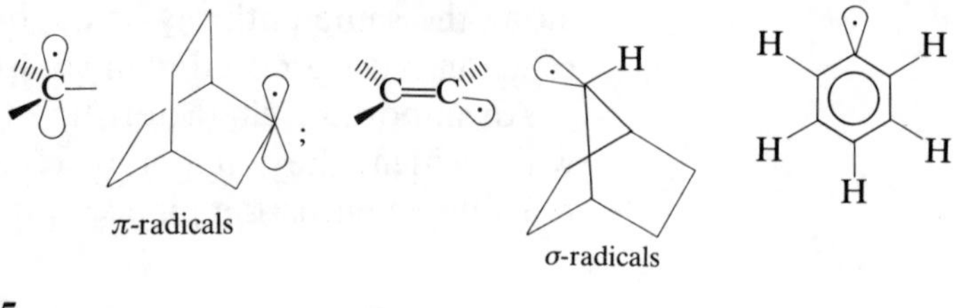

π-radicals σ-radicals

Fig. 9.5

radicals can exist in both π- and σ-states. A good example is the succinimidyl radical which is believed to exist in two electronic states of different reactivity (Fig. 9.6). The upper σ-state is much more reactive than the ground π-state. Thus the σ-state will abstract hydrogen from alkanes and add to olefinic double bonds, reactions not shown by the π-radical.

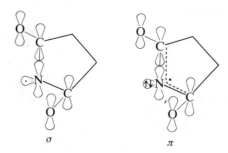

Fig. 9.6 The two electronic states of the succinimidyl radical

Carbanions

The chemistry of carbanions has been discussed in earlier chapters. The ground state of most carbanions is pyramidal, but like the ammonia molecule they invert at normal temperatures:

Carbenes

The reactive species, CH_2, called carbene, can exist in two electronic states, singlet and triplet. Photolysis of a precursor such as diazomethane or ketene yields the upper more reactive singlet state which adds in an exclusively *cis* manner to double bonds and inserts unselectively into carbon–hydrogen bonds. In the presence of an inert gas the lower-energy triplet is selective in its insertion and adds non-stereospecifically to double bonds.

There is strong evidence that the energy states of dichlorocarbene are reversed and the singlet is the ground state. This is because the full p-atomic orbitals of the chlorine atom can interact with the vacant 2p orbital of the carbon.

77

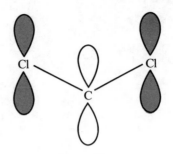

Benzyne

Benzyne (bis-dehydrobenzene) is formed by a variety of

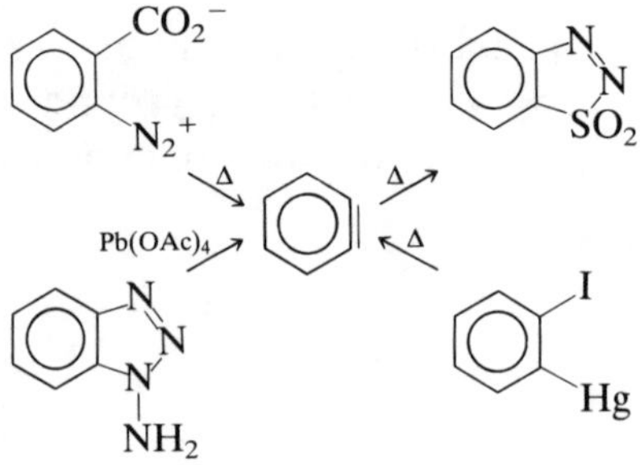

thermolysis reactions involving *ortho*-substituted benzene derivatives and also by the reaction of aryl halides with very strong
bases:

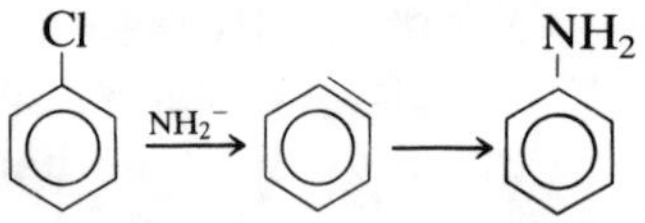

The overlap between the sp^2 lobes in benzyne is very small but
this accounts for its great reactivity:

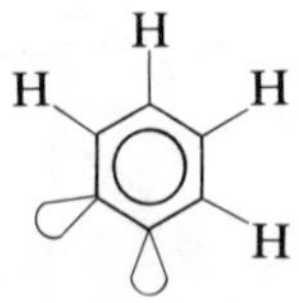

As well as combining with itself, reaction path (A), benzyne
behaves as a dienophile in a Diels–Alder reaction (B). For
reaction path B see Chapter 10.

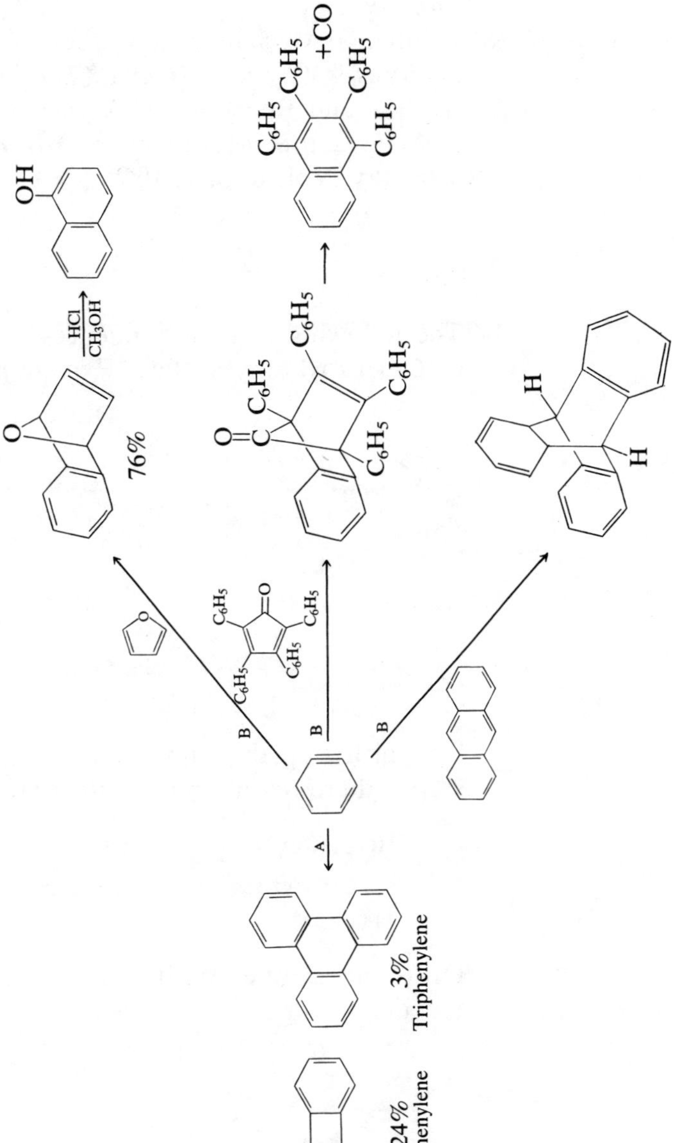

Fig. 9.7 Behaviour of benzyne in a Diels–Alder reaction

Further reading

Reactive Intermediates In Organic Chemistry, N. S. Isaacs, Wiley, New York, 1974.

Carbene Chemistry, 2nd edn, W. Kirmse, Academic Press, New York, 1971.

'Structure and Mechanism in Carbene Chemistry', D. Bethell, in *Advances in Physical Organic Chemistry*, Vol. 7, p. 153, 1969.

'Formation and Reactions of Arynes at High Temperature', E. K. Fields and S. Meyerson, in *Advances in Physical Organic Chemistry*, Vol. 6, p. 1, 1968.

Problems

1 The following reaction sequences yield the two enantiomers of *O*-benzoyl ethyl lactate. Explain how this is achieved.

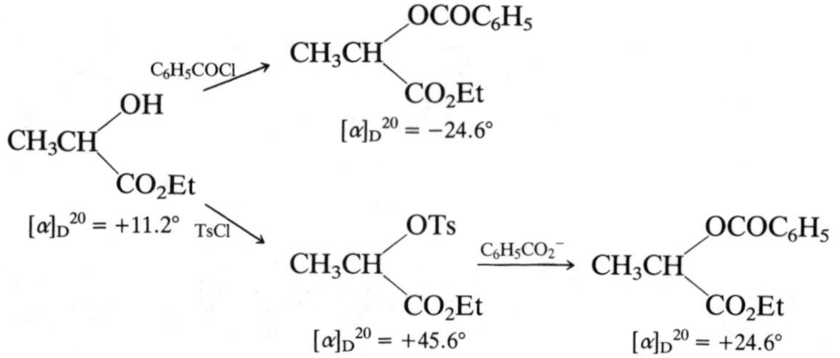

2 At which step does inversion occur, and why in the other step is there retention of configuration?

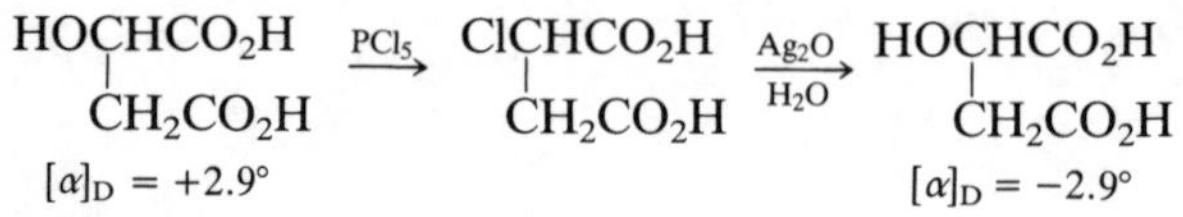

3 Draw the frontier orbitals in the following rearrangement reaction.

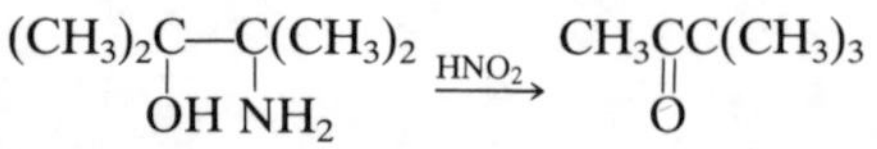

$$(CH_3)_2C\!-\!C(CH_3)_2 \quad \xrightarrow{\text{HNO}_2} \quad CH_3CC(CH_3)_3$$
$$\underset{\text{OH NH}_2}{} \qquad \underset{\text{O}}{}$$

4 Hydrogen abstraction from the following yield 'σ' and 'π' radicals; which gives which?

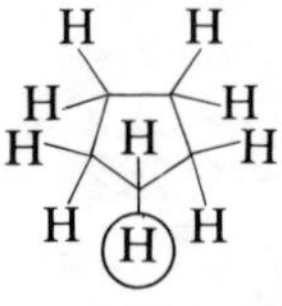

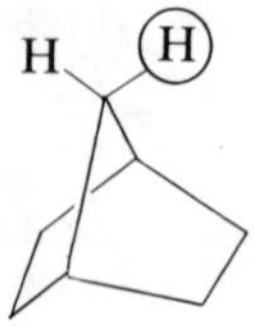

5 During bromination of cyclohexane with *N*-bromosuccinimide

$$\underset{\substack{\text{NBr}}}{\text{(succinimide ring with two C=O)}} \qquad \text{some} \qquad CH_3CH_2-C\overset{O}{\underset{N=C=O}{\diagdown}}$$

can be isolated. What does this fact imply about the nature of the intermediate succinimidyl radical?

10 Alternant Hydrocarbons and Aromaticity

The energies of the π-molecular orbitals of conjugated molecules like butadiene (Fig. 10.1) occur in pairs with their energies equal to $(\alpha \pm x\beta)$, where α and β are constants. For each bonding orbital of an energy $\alpha - x\beta$ there is a corresponding antibonding orbital of energy $\alpha + x\beta$. In the chapter on addition reactions we saw that butadiene and similar molecules underwent 1,4- as well as 1,2-addition. The π-molecular orbitals are extended over the whole molecule and the same applies to the π-molecular orbitals of hexatriene and octatetraene. Both these molecules can undergo conjugate addition (i.e. 1,6- and 1,8-addition respectively).

The radicals allyl $\overset{\displaystyle .}{\overbrace{CH_2\!-\!CH\!-\!CH_2}}$ and pentadienyl $\overbrace{CH_2\!-\!CH\!-\!CH\!-\!CH\!-\!CH_2}$ have the same arrangement of their π-orbitals (i.e. they occur in pairs of energy $\alpha \pm x\beta$) but because there is an odd number of carbon atoms in the conjugate chain, there must be a non-bonding orbital of energy with $x = 0$, (i.e. of energy α). Furthermore, because of the pairing properties of π-molecular orbitals of conjugated chains there will be a node at every alternate carbon atom in the non-bonding orbital. This has important consequences for the unpaired electron of allyl (or pentadienyl) which will occupy this non-bonding orbital. If an electron is added to the allyl radical to form the allyl anion, the negative charge will appear equally at the terminal carbon atoms; similarly, if the unpaired electron is removed from the allyl radical the resulting cation (Fig. 10.2) will have the positive charge equally distributed between the terminal carbon atoms.

In the pentadienyl anion, the negative charge will be centred on the carbon atoms 1, 3 and 5, and of course the positive charge in the pentadienyl cation will occur at the same sites and similarly for the unpaired electron (Fig. 10.3).

These ions are represented in resonance theory as two or three canonical forms:

$$\overset{+}{C}H_2\!-\!CH\!=\!CH_2 \quad \longleftrightarrow \quad CH_2\!=\!CH\!-\!\overset{+}{C}H_2$$

Resonance structures for the allyl cation

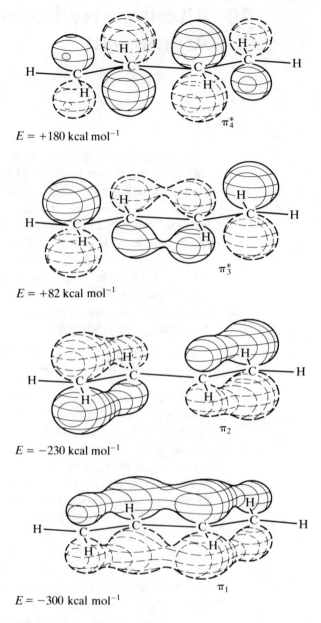

$E = +180 \text{ kcal mol}^{-1}$ — π_4^*

$E = +82 \text{ kcal mol}^{-1}$ — π_3^*

$E = -230 \text{ kcal mol}^{-1}$ — π_2

$E = -300 \text{ kcal mol}^{-1}$ — π_1

Fig. 10.1 1,3-Butadiene (transoid)

$$\dot{C}H_2\!-\!CH\!=\!CH\!-\!CH\!=\!CH_2 \longleftrightarrow CH_2\!=\!CH\!-\!\dot{C}H\!-\!CH\!=\!CH_2 \longleftrightarrow CH_2\!=\!CH\!-\!CH\!=\!CH\!-\!\dot{C}H_2$$

Resonance structures for the pentadienyl radical

This delocalization of π-electrons is associated with a lowering of the energy. Thus the total energy of the occupied π-orbitals

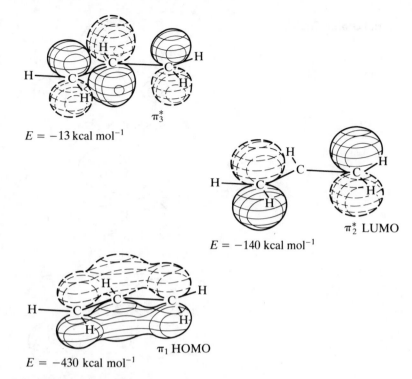

$E = -13\,\text{kcal mol}^{-1}$

π_3^*

π_2^* LUMO

$E = -140\,\text{kcal mol}^{-1}$

π_1 HOMO

$E = -430\,\text{kcal mol}^{-1}$

Fig. 10.2 Allyl cation

of butadiene is lower than the energy of two isolated ethylenic double bonds, although the HOMO of the butadiene is of higher energy than the HOMO of ethene.

Further delocalization of π-type electrons occurs in aromatic hydrocarbons (Fig. 10.4). In all the cyclic polyenes (C_nH_n), the π-molecular orbitals occur in degenerate pairs except the lowest π-orbital and, in the cyclic polyenes with an even number of carbon atoms the highest π-orbital. Cyclopropenyl has three π-orbitals, one bonding and two anti-bonding which are degenerate (i.e. of the same energy). There are three electrons to go into these orbitals, two into the bonding orbital and one into one of the antibonding orbitals. If an electron is removed from the cyclopropenyl radical, the resulting cyclopropenium cation has a completely delocalized HOMO extending over the three carbon atoms occupied by a pair of electrons. Cyclopropenium compounds have been prepared, for example 1,2,3-triphenylcyclopropenium fluoroborate:

C_6H_5 C_6H_5

BF_4^-

C_6H_5

A cyclopropenium salt

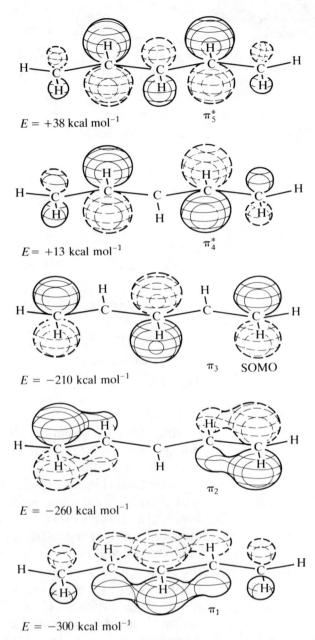

$E = +38 \text{ kcal mol}^{-1}$ $\qquad \pi_5^*$

$E = +13 \text{ kcal mol}^{-1}$ $\qquad \pi_4^*$

$E = -210 \text{ kcal mol}^{-1}$ $\qquad \pi_3$ SOMO

$E = -260 \text{ kcal mol}^{-1}$ $\qquad \pi_2$

$E = -300 \text{ kcal mol}^{-1}$ $\qquad \pi_1$

Fig. 10.3 Pentadienyl radical (π-orbitals only). Symmetry: C_{2v}

Square cyclobutadiene (C_4H_4) would have four 'π-orbitals', a bonding orbital, two degenerate non-bonding orbitals and an antibonding orbital. Four electrons need to be placed into these four orbitals; two would go into the bonding orbital and one each with parallel spins into the degenerate non-bonding orbital (Hund's rule). The fallacy of this argument is that there is no reason to expect cyclobutadiene to be square, indeed an

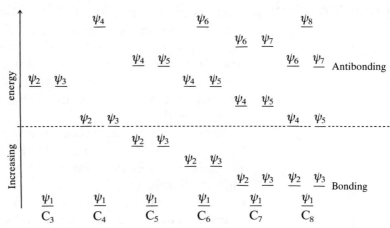

Fig. 10.4 Energy levels of the π-orbitals of cyclic molecules C_nH_n ($n = 3$ to $n = 8$)

oblong shape with the four π-electrons in two isolated 'double bonds' is likely to be of lower energy (Jahn–Teller theorem). Experiment confirms that cyclobutadiene behaves as a very strained cyclo-olefin and not as a biradical.

Cyclopentadiene is a relatively acidic hydrocarbon and the anion (Fig. 10.5), formed by treatment of cyclopentadiene with

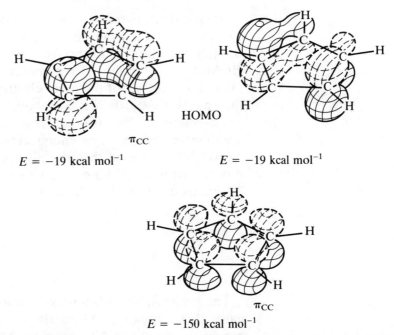

Fig. 10.5 Bonding π-orbitals of the cyclopentadienyl anion (N.B. there are σ C—C orbitals $E = -81.5\,\mathrm{kcal\,mol^{-1}}$, a degenerate pair $E = -132\,\mathrm{kcal\,mol^{-1}}$, also a degenerate pair between the upper π levels and the lowest π level, *not* shown.)

a strong base, has three π C—C orbitals which are delocalized over the five carbon atoms. The uppermost π-orbitals are a degenerate pair and are the highest occupied molecular orbitals. The lowest energy π C—C orbital is of much lower energy and there are four σ C—C orbitals (not shown) occurring as degenerate pairs between the two HOMOs and the lower π C—C orbital.

Benzene is the archetype aromatic compound. Figure 10.6 shows the six π-molecular orbitals, three bonding and three antibonding. It is most important to appreciate that there are four σ-orbitals (σ, C—H, σ, C—C, and a degenerate pair σ C—C, C—H) not shown between the upper two degenerate π-levels shown and the lower π-level shown. However, the upper bonding π-levels are the highest occupied molecular orbitals in the ground state of benzene.

The chemistry of benzene is characterized by 'addition-with-elimination' reactions in which the six delocalized π-electrons are retained in the final product.

At first sight, pyridine (Fig. 10.7) has very much the same de-localized electron arrangement. The uppermost two occupied π-orbitals are close in energy, corresponding to the degenerate HOMO pair in benzene. Their energy is much lower, correspond-ing to the presence of the more electronegative nitrogen atom in the ring. However, there is an important difference in the electron arrangement in the two molecules. In pyridine there is a non-bonding orbital of an energy close to that of the two upper π-levels. This means that the nitrogen atom can take part in bonding with a LUMO-gen (e.g. a proton) while the molecule retains its delocalized π-electron system.

The five-membered heterocyclic compounds pyrrole and furan have three bonding π-orbitals like those of benzene and pyridine, and furan like pyridine has a non-bonding orbital centred on the heteroatom. In pyrrole, the energies of the uppermost bonding pair of orbitals are close, in contrast to those of furan. The chemistry of pyrrole shows greater similarity to

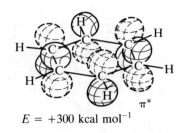

$E = +300 \text{ kcal mol}^{-1}$

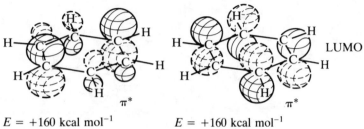

$E = +160 \text{ kcal mol}^{-1}$ $E = +160 \text{ kcal mol}^{-1}$

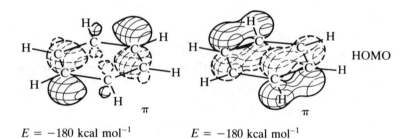

$E = -180 \text{ kcal mol}^{-1}$ $E = -180 \text{ kcal mol}^{-1}$

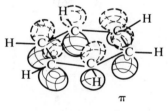

$E = -300 \text{ kcal mol}^{-1}$

Fig. 10.6 π-electron levels of benzene (N.B. σ-electron levels are *not* shown)

that of benzene than that of furan. Furan (Fig. 10.8) undergoes cyclic addition reactions (see Chapter 12) and in general takes part in addition reactions much more readily than pyrrole (Fig. 10.9). The electrons in the non-bonding orbital of furan are very tightly bound and furan is not a strong base, in contrast to pyridine, where the energy gap between the upper π-levels and the non-bonding orbital is relatively small. Pyridine is a strong base.

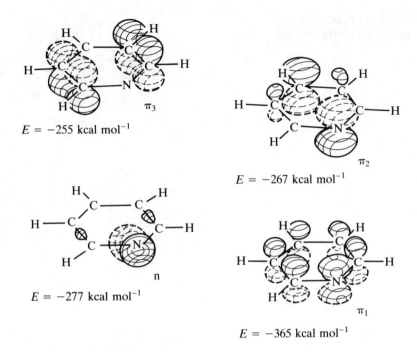

Fig. 10.7 Pyridine: three π-molecular orbitals and one non-bonding orbital (N.B. There is a σ-orbital between the n and the π_1-orbitals)

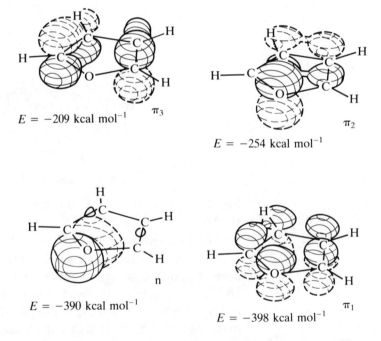

Fig. 10.8 Furan: the three bonding π-orbitals and the non-bonding orbital (N.B. There are σ-orbitals not shown)

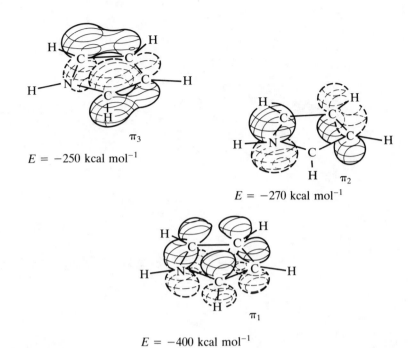

π_3

$E = -250 \text{ kcal mol}^{-1}$

π_2

$E = -270 \text{ kcal mol}^{-1}$

π_1

$E = -400 \text{ kcal mol}^{-1}$

Fig. 10.9 Pyrrole: bonding π-orbitals only (N.B. There are three σ-orbitals between π_2 and π_1)

Further reading

Non-benzenoid Conjugated Carbocyclic Compounds, D. M. G. Lloyd, Elsevier, Amsterdam, 1984.
Aromaticity, P. J. Garratt, McGraw-Hill, Maidenhead, 1971.

Problems

1 Explain why bicyclo-octatriene which has six π electrons shows no 'aromatic' properties.

?

2 Why is cyclopentadiene an acidic substance compared with butadiene?

3 Explain in orbital terms why the chemistry of pyridine and benzene is so different.

11 The Reactions of Benzenoid Compounds

Benzene and its derivatives are particularly characterized by the fact they undergo 'substitution' rather than 'addition' reactions. Perhaps the reactions are best called 'addition-with-elimination' reactions since the primary step is addition. There are three types of addition reaction: cationic, radical and anionic:

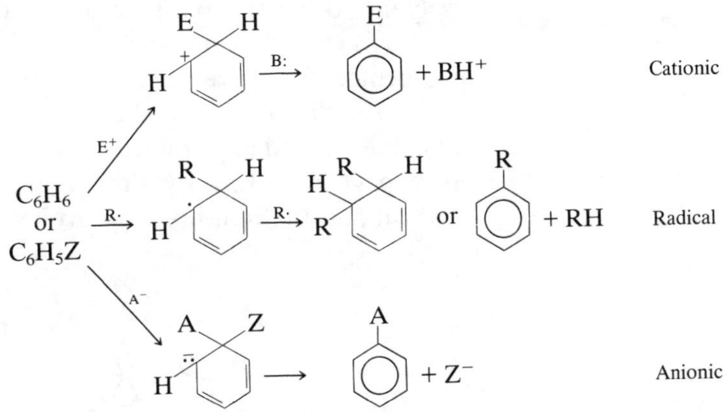

The most important of these addition-with-elimination reactions is the cationic, in which the aromatic compound behaves as the HOMO-gen.

Cationic substitution in aromatic compounds

The nitration of aromatic compounds involves attack by the nitronium ion. The range of reactivity is enormous as illustrated in Table 11.1.

$$NO_2^+ + C_6H_6 \longrightarrow [C_6H_6NO_2]^+ \longrightarrow C_6H_5NO_2 + (H^+)$$

The relative rate data are nothing more than intelligent guesses. For example nitrobenzene is nitrated in concentrated sulfuric acid medium and anisole in acetic anhydride, so that direct comparison is impossible.

Very similar data is also available for chlorination of the same compounds.

Table 11.1 The orientation and approximate relative rates of nitration of mono-substituted benzenes C_6H_5X

X	Orientation			Relative rate $(C_6H_6 = 1)$	
	o	m	p		
CH_3O	72	—	28	10^3	Donor
CH_3	58	5	37	10	Repeller
Cl	30	1	69	10^{-2}	Attracting donor
CCl_3	7	65	28	10^{-3}	Attractor
NO_2	6	93	1	10^{-4}	Acceptor

Just as the π-orbitals of conjugated double bonds in a linear polyene occur in pairs, one bonding and one anti-bonding $(\alpha \pm x\beta)$, so the same treatment can be applied to the benzene molecule. We have seen that in a linear conjugated ion or radical with an odd number of atoms in the conjugated chain, like the pentadienyl radical, there is a non-bonding orbital (α) (see page 83). Exactly similar arguments apply to the benzyl radical and the non-bonding orbital can be represented thus:

$\updownarrow$ = node

The HOMO of benzyl

If an electron is added to the benzyl radical it will go into the HOMO (NBO) and the resulting negative charge will appear at the two *ortho*-positions and the *para*-position as well as on the exocyclic carbon atom:

Charge distribution in the benzyl anion (Hückel calculation)

The electron distribution of the phenoxide ion is very similar to that of the benzyl anion. However any substituent with non-bonding electron pairs (e.g. H_2N-, CH_3O-, $F-$, $Cl-$, $Br-$, $HS-$, etc.) will interact with the benzene nucleus in the same way. Thus even though there is no overall charge, the

electron density in the HOMO of such an aromatic compound
(i.e. one with a substituent having non-bonding electron pairs)
will be highest at the positions *ortho-* and *para-* to the 'donor'
substituent, and usually the reaction is faster than with benzene.
Halogen atoms have non-bonded electrons which can interact
with adjacent vacant orbitals, but they are also much more electronegative than carbon. The net effect is that the halogens
direct *ortho-para* but the reaction is slower than with benzenes.

If instead of non-bonding electron pairs a substituent has
low-lying unoccupied orbitals which can accept electrons from
the benzene ring (e.g. NO_2—, RCO—, CN—, etc.) these will in
turn come from the *ortho-* and *para*-positions. A benzene ring
with an acceptor group as a substituent will be deactivated to

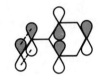

Acceptor group

addition-with-elimination reactions like nitration and attack will
occur preferentially *meta-* to the substituent.

Substituents which lack orbitals of π-symmetry and which
cannot interact with the π-orbitals of a benzene ring can only
exert an inductive effect. The frontier orbital of toluene is
shown below:

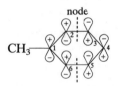

An attacking electrophile approaching the HOMO of toluene
will interact with atoms 1 and 2, or 3 and 4, or 4 and 5, or 1 and
6 (but not with atoms 2 and 3 or 5 and 6). If the methyl
substituent exerts a steric effect inhibiting attack at the
1-position, it is clear that attack will be favoured at the *ortho-*
and *para*-positions and to a lesser extent at the *meta*-position.
Although, in the ground state, the methyl group can be regarded as an electron repeller, in a reaction involving electron
demand, the methyl group can become a donor through hyperconjugation.

Hyperconjugation is the term given to the process by which a
group such as a methyl group interacts with an unsaturated
system as though it possessed electrons of π symmetry. We have

to break down the orbitals of the CH_3 group in such a way that we obtain the components of π symmetry. If we take an orientation of the methyl group relative to the benzene ring as shown:

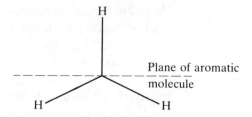

The orientation of the methyl group relative to the aromatic ring

then one of the group orbitals of the methyl group, the π_z orbital, has a nodal plane roughly in line with the nodal plane of the π orbitals of the benzene ring, allowing delocalization between the methyl group and the benzene ring.

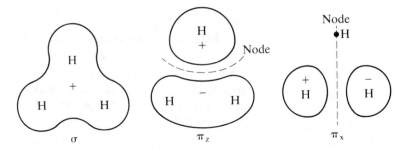

(a) The group orbitals of the hydrogen atoms in a methyl substituent

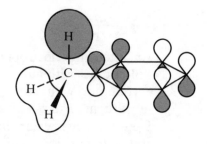

(b) CH_3 π_z: benzene π_3 interaction

The π-inductive effect of the methyl group will slightly increase electron density of the HOMO at alternate positions and will therefore facilitate cationic attack at the *ortho*- and *para*-positions. Similarly an electron attracting substituent (e.g.

CF_3—) will slightly decrease the electron density of the HOMO at alternate positions and cationic attack will occur preferentially at the *meta*-position, the reaction being slower than with benzene.

Although conventional resonance theory can account satisfactorily for the gross orientation (i.e. *ortho-* and *para-* or *meta-*) observed in most cationic addition-with-elimination reactions, it can give no explanation of the large differences in the ratio of attack at the *ortho-* and *para*-positions. Thus as Table 11.1 shows, methoxy (CH_3O—), methyl (CH_3—) and chlorine (Cl—) all direct nitration to the *ortho-* and *para*-positions but the relative rates of attack at the *ortho-* to *para*-positions vary significantly: *ortho/para* $\times 2 = 1.3$ (CH_3O), 0.78 (CH_3) and 0.22 (Cl). (N.B. this is not the order expected on steric considerations).

Table 11.2 The orientation of cationic attack on toluene by different reagents

	%			*ortho*/2 × *para*
	o	*m*	*p*	
$C_6H_5CH_3$ + (HNO_3 in CH_3NO_2)	61	1.9	36.4	0.84
$C_6H_5CH_3$ + (CH_3Br; $AlBr_3$)	49.8	20.3	29.5	0.68
$C_6H_5CH_3$ + ($C_6H_5CH_2Br$; $GaBr$)	41.1	19.5	39.5	0.52
$C_6H_5CH_3$ + ($H_2SO_4 + H_2O$)	36	4.5	59	0.31
$C_6H_5CH_3$ + (CH_2O; HCl; $ZnCl_2$; AcOH)	34.7	1.3	64.0	0.27
$C_6H_5CH_3$ + (C_5H_5COCl; $AlCl_3$; $C_6H_5NO_2$)	7.2	1.1	91.7	0.04
$C_6H_5CH_3$ + (CH_3COCl; $AlCl_3$; $C_2H_2Cl_2$)	1.2	2.3	97.6	0.006

Table 11.2 shows there is a large variation in the *ortho/para* ratio ($> \times 10^2$). The differences cannot be attributed to steric effects since the first and the last reagents, namely $O{=}\overset{+}{N}{=}O$ and $CH_3{-}\overset{+}{C}{=}O$ have very similar steric requirements. The increasing proportion of *meta*-product towards the top of the Table for all but nitration is probably due to the increasing reactivity of the cationic species (e.g. CH_3^+ will be much more reactive and less selective than CH_3CO^+). The acetylium ion (CH_3CO^+) can be formed in solution without any Lewis acid like $AlCl_3$ etc., and it proves very selective in its reaction with

anisole (in sharp contrast to the reaction of the nitronium ion (NO_2^+) with anisole).

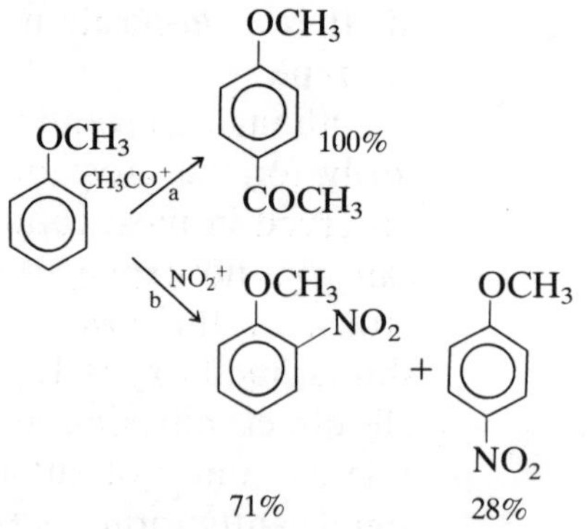

(a) $HClO_4$(or CF_3CO_2H) + $(CH_3CO)_2O$
(b) HNO_3 + $(CH_3CO)_2O$

The high rate of attack at the *ortho*-position corresponds to attack at the site carrying the greatest negative charge, i.e. 'charge control'. In contrast a high rate of attack at the *para*-position corresponds to attack at the site carrying the highest electron density in the HOMO, i.e. 'orbital control'. A common suggestion that the high yield of *ortho*-product from the nitration of anisole in acetic anhydride is due to an oxygen bridge to the carbonyl, cannot be sustained. When the *ortho/para*

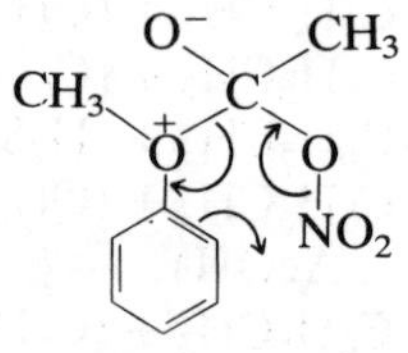

Fig. 11.1 Fallacious 'explanation' of the high rate of *ortho*-attack in the nitration of anisole

ratios for the nitration of toluene and anisole are compared in different media the preference for *ortho*-attack on anisole is only slightly greater than it is for toluene.

Examination of Table 11.2 shows that ions which have particularly high ionization potentials (CH_3^+, 9.9 eV, −228 kcal mol^{-1}; NO_2^+, 9.8 eV, −226 kcal mol^{-1}) are those which favour *ortho*-attack, i.e. 'charge control'. In contrast the acetylium ion which has a low ionization potential (CH_3CO^+, 8.1 eV, −187 kcal mol^{-1}) is relatively unreactive and favours exclusive *para*-attack, i.e. 'orbital control'. Thus for toluene, approximate molecular orbital theories show the 2-position as carrying the highest negative charge whereas the 4-position has the highest electron density in the HOMO.

Other common examples of the change from charge control to orbital control include

(*a*) the nitration and nitrosation of phenol:

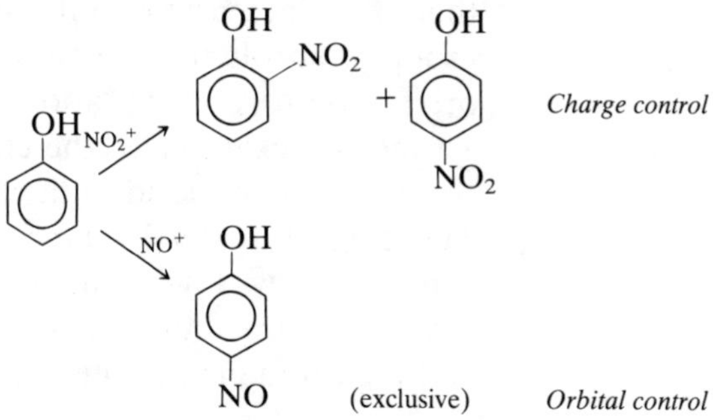

Charge control

Orbital control

(*b*) the nitration and nitrosation of dimethylaniline

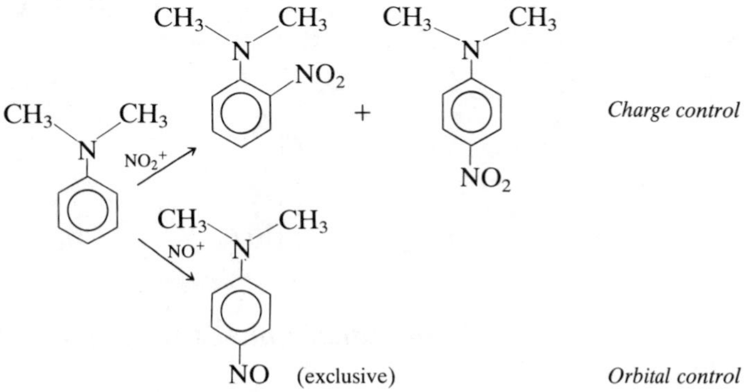

Charge control

Orbital control

(*c*) the diazo-coupling of naphthol sulfonic acids

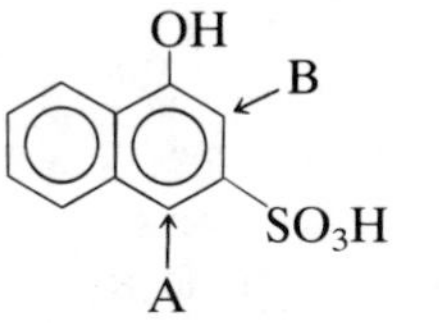

'A' = 2,4(NO$_2$)$_2$C$_6$H$_3\overset{+}{N}$≡N   *Charge control*
'B' = C$_6$H$_5\overset{+}{N}$≡N   *Orbital control*

(*d*) the acylation of toluene using acylium ions of increasing electronegativity

$$RCOCl + C_6H_5CH_3 \xrightarrow{\ AlCl_3\ } RCOC_6H_4CH_3 \ (o, m \text{ and } p)$$

R	*o*	*m*	*p*
CH$_3$	2	2	96
ClCH$_2$	11	2	87
Cl$_2$CH	17	3	80

The increasing chlorine presence in the attacking acylium ion would on steric grounds be expected to decrease the *ortho*-attack. Instead the increasing polarity of the transition state increases the importance of 'charge control'. Steric effects are important but the fact that in this case charge difference rather than the increasing bulk of the chloro- and dichloro-methyl groups controls the reaction, emphasizes the important role that orbital control plays in cationic addition-with-elimination reactions.

Another example of the change from charge control to orbital control is to be found in the benzylation of toluene and benzene. The largest *ortho*/2 × *para* ratios are associated with charge control, and low toluene/benzene selectivity while a low *ortho*/2 × *para* ratio is associated with increasing orbital control and high toluene/benzene selectivity.

$$p\text{XC}_6\text{H}_4\text{CH}_2\text{Cl} + \text{C}_6\text{H}_6(\text{CH}_3\text{C}_6\text{H}_5) \xrightarrow{\text{TiCl}_4} p\text{XC}_6\text{H}_5\text{CH}_2\text{C}_6\text{H}_5$$
$$(p\text{XC}_6\text{H}_5\text{CH}_2\text{C}_6\text{H}_4\text{CH}_3 \ o, \ m \ \text{and} \ p)$$

X	$k_{\text{C}_7\text{H}_8}/k_{\text{C}_6\text{H}_6}$	*ortho*/2 × *para*
NO$_2$	2.5	0.87
Cl	6.2	0.37
H	6.3	0.37
CH$_3$	29	0.24
CH$_3$O	97	0.20

Free radical substitution in aromatic compounds

The reaction of free radicals with aromatic compounds is often a complicated process because the initially formed adduct radical can undergo a number of subsequent reactions.

The orientation for the phenylation of some substituted benzenes is shown in Table 11.3.

Compared with the cationic attack on mono-substituted benzenes the data in the above table shows phenyl radical attack to be very unselective. Some substituents may be expected to stabilize the initial adduct radical. However the canonical structures of resonance theory show that delocalization of the

Table 11.3 The phenylation of mono-substituted benzenes (C_6H_5R + $C_6H_5\cdot$)

R	Relative rate*	Orientation		
		ortho	*meta*	*para*
CH_3O	2.71	55.6	26.9	17.5
Cl	2.20	59.0	25.0	26.0
CH_3	2.58	60.9	16.1	23.0
NO_2	2.44	62.5	9.8	27.7

* Relative rate $C_6H_6 = 1$

unpaired electron onto the oxygen atom in anisole (or to the chlorine atom in chlorobenzene) requires the formation of a

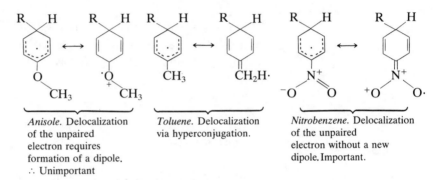

Anisole. Delocalization of the unpaired electron requires formation of a dipole. ∴ Unimportant

Toluene. Delocalization via hyperconjugation.

Nitrobenzene. Delocalization of the unpaired electron without a new dipole. Important.

dipole. Such structures which involve separation of charge therefore make negligible contribution to the ground state of the adduct radical.

Anionic substitution in aromatic compounds

Whereas the more familiar cationic substitution of aromatic compounds involves the HOMO of the arene, anionic substitution involves the LUMO. However we can treat the mono-substituted benzenes in the same way, i.e. look at the coefficients of the non-bonding orbital for the benzyl cation. If we replace the CH_2^+ group by a nitro-group, some build up of charge at the *ortho-* and *para*-positions is to be expected.

$$CH_2 + \tfrac{4}{7}$$
$$+\tfrac{1}{7} \qquad +\tfrac{1}{7}$$
$$+\tfrac{1}{7}$$

Charge distribution in the benzyl cation

Figure 11.2 shows the relative rates of substitution by NaOCH$_3$ in methanol, of four *para*-substituted 2-nitro-chlorobenzenes.

Relative rates of

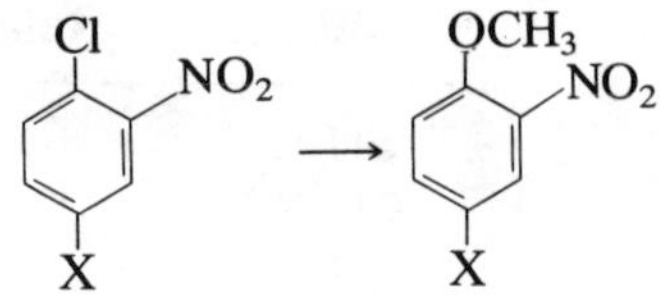

where

X = H   CH$_3$ Cl   CF$_3$
1.0   0.26   11.2   35.7

Fig. 11.2 The relative rates of the displacement of Cl— by CH$_3$O— in substituted 2-nitro-chlorobenzene

The data shows that a methyl group which repels electrons retards the reaction while the trifluoromethyl group which strongly attracts electrons greatly enhances the rate of substitution.

Conclusions

Pictorial orbital theory is thus able to account for the orientation of substitution in the 'addition-with-elimination' reactions of the arenes more comprehensively than simple resonance theory. In particular it is able to explain changes in the *ortho:para* ratio of cationic substitution, in terms of the change of charge control to orbital control. Free radical substitution of aromatic compounds is most easily accounted for in resonance theory, but anionic substitution is again amenable to treatment in orbital terms.

Further reading

Electrophilic Substitution in Benzenoid Compounds, R. O. C. Norman and R. Taylor, Elsevier, Amsterdam, 1965.
Fricdel–Crafts and Related Reactions, ed. G. A. Olah, Interscience, New York, 1964.

Problems

1 Draw the HOMO of the phenoxide anion.

2 Discuss the following observation:

3 Explain the following observations for homolytic arylation in terms of polar effects in the aryl radical.

Substrate	Radical	% o	m	p	Ratio $(o + p)/m$
PhCl	Ph·	56.9	25.6	17.5	2.9
	C_6F_5·	64.7	20.6	14.7	3.9
PhNO$_2$	Ph·	62.5	9.8	27.7	9.2
	C_6F_5·	20.8	53.4	25.8	0.87

12 Pericyclic Reactions

The Diels–Alder reaction

In Chapter 7 we depicted the addition of an anion to a carbonyl double bond as involving the interaction of the HOMO of the anion with the LUMO (π^*) of the carbonyl bond. Similarly we depicted the addition of a cation to one olefinic double bond as involving the LUMO of the cation with the HOMO (π) of the double bond. Simple addition reactions of this kind involve three atomic centres simultaneously. In this chapter we are concerned with processes which involve concerted reaction in a cyclic transition state. The best known example is the Diels–Alder reaction; at one time it was called a 'no mechanism reaction' but Woodward and Hoffmann showed that if the interaction between the frontier orbitals was considered, the course and stereochemistry of these reactions could be elucidated. Thus the interaction of ethene and butadiene can be depicted as shown in Fig. 12.1.

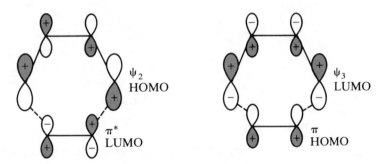

Fig. 12.1 The interaction of the frontier orbitals of ethene, and *cis*-1,3-butadiene

The diagram shows that if ethene (in practice a substituted ethene) and *cisoid*-butadiene approach with their molecular planes parallel, one above the other, there is the possibility of a bonding interaction between them. The highest occupied orbital of butadiene interacts with the lowest unoccupied orbital of the ethene and simultaneously the lowest unoccupied orbital of butadiene interacts with the highest occupied orbital of the ethene. In sharp contrast, any attempt to bring two ethene molecules together results in an antibonding interaction (Fig. 12.2).

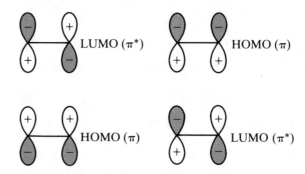

LUMO (π^*)   HOMO (π)

HOMO (π)   LUMO (π^*)

Fig. 12.2 The interaction of the frontier orbitals of two ethene molecules

These cyclic reactions are very common and include systems containing triple bonds and heteroatoms (Fig. 12.3). Examina-

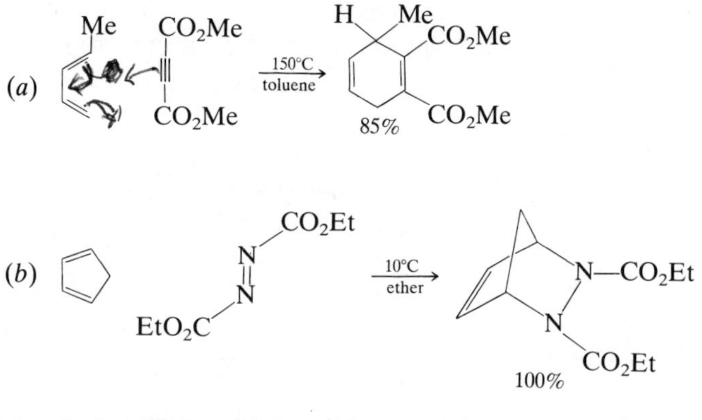

(a)

Me CO$_2$Me

CO$_2$Me

$\xrightarrow[\text{toluene}]{150°C}$

H Me
CO$_2$Me

CO$_2$Me

85%

(b)

CO$_2$Et
N
‖
N
EtO$_2$C

$\xrightarrow[\text{ether}]{10°C}$

N—CO$_2$Et
N
CO$_2$Et

100%

Fig. 12.3 Cycloaddition (a) involving a triple bond and (b) involving heteroatoms

tion of the reactions we have described make it apparent that for a cyclic reaction to be 'symmetry allowed' (i.e. for there to be a bonding interaction throughout the reaction) the number of atoms in the cyclic process must be 2k where k is odd (e.g. k = 3 for the Diels–Alder reaction). For example cyclohexadiene undergoes cyclic addition with tropolone (cycloheptatrienone). There are ten carbon atoms involved in the addition (asterisked), i.e. 2k = 10 : k = 5.

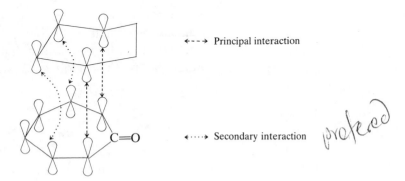

4:6-Cycloaddition ($2k$ atoms involved; $k = 5$, i.e. odd)

Endo-addition is preferred over exo-addition because of secondary orbital–orbital interaction shown as dotted lines (Fig. 12.4).

←--→ Principal interaction

←····→ Secondary interaction

Fig. 12.4

1,3-Dipolar reactions or 3:2 cyclizations

Closely related to the Diels–Alder cyclic addition reactions are the 1,3-dipolar cycloadditions (Fig. 12.5). These are reactions involving six electrons in π-equivalent orbitals extending over five (instead of six) atoms. The three-atom component can be one of a very large group of 1,3-dipolar molecules, e.g.

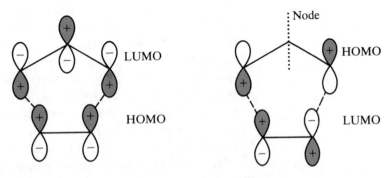

Fig. 12.5 1,3-Dipolar additions or 3:2 cyclization

$$CH_2=\overset{+}{\overset{\cdot\cdot}{N}}=\bar{N}; \quad R-N=\overset{+}{N}=\bar{N}; \quad R-C\equiv\overset{+}{N}-\bar{O}; \quad O=\overset{+}{\overset{\cdot\cdot}{O}}-\bar{O};$$

and also $(MnO_4)^-$; (OsO_4) etc.

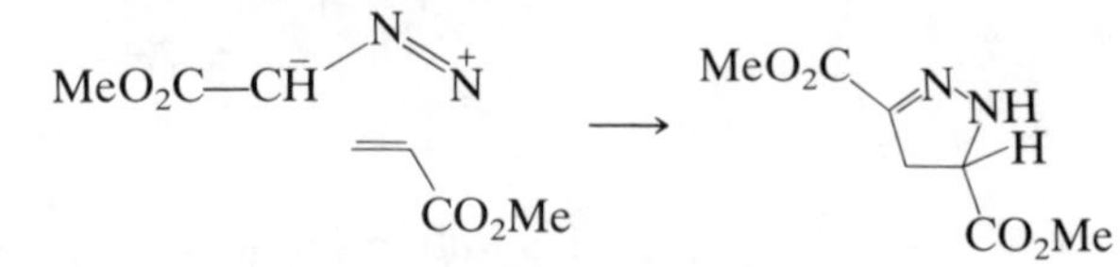

1,3-Dipolar addition of diazomethane to methyl acrylate

Electrocyclic reactions (Fig. 12.6)

When *trans,cis,trans*-octa-2,4,6-triene is heated, it undergoes cyclization to yield *cis*-1,6-dimethylcyclohexa-3,5-diene, but on irradiation with ultra-violet light the same triene yields the *trans*-1,6-dimethylcyclohexa-3,5-diene.

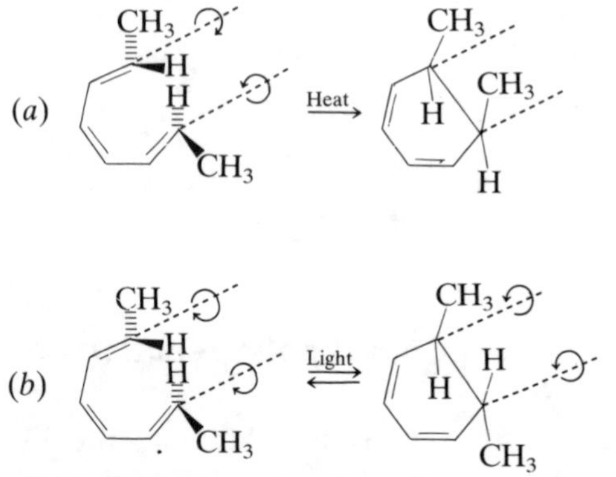

Fig. 12.6 Electrocyclic reactions. (*a*) *Disrotatory*—Thermal cyclization of dimethylhexatriene; (*b*) *Conrotatory*—Photochemical cyclization of dimethylhexatriene

Both these reactions are stereospecific. In the photochemical cyclization of the hexatriene (which is reversible) the terminal groups rotate the same way, i.e. the reaction is *conrotatory*, like the thermal ring opening of the cyclobutene. In the thermal ring closure of the hexatriene, however, the terminal groups rotate in opposite directions and the reaction is called *disrotatory*. The *conrotatory* mode has a C_2 axis while the *disrotatory* mode has a mirror plane (Fig. 12.7). We can depict the relevant 'frontier orbitals' as shown in Fig. 12.8.

From our knowledge of the pairing properties of Hückel type π-orbitals (see page 32), we know that the number of nodes in

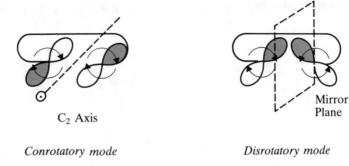

C$_2$ Axis

Conrotatory mode

Mirror Plane

Disrotatory mode

Fig. 12.7

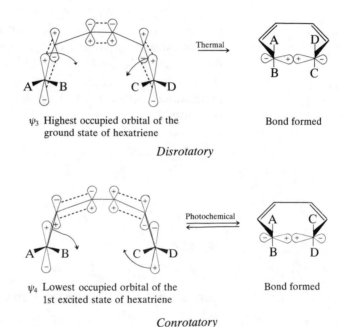

ψ_3 Highest occupied orbital of the ground state of hexatriene

Bond formed

Disrotatory

ψ_4 Lowest occupied orbital of the 1st excited state of hexatriene

Bond formed

Conrotatory

Fig. 12.8

the highest bonding orbital of an even alternant (i.e. a linear) polyene will be $k - 1$; where $2k$ is the number of atoms in the chain. If k is odd, the symmetry of the highest bonding orbital is such that a *disrotatory* process will lead to a bonding σ-bond between the terminal carbon atoms on ring closure. If k is even, the symmetry of the highest bonding orbital is such that a *conrotatory* process is necessary to produce a bonding σ-bond between the terminal carbon atoms on ring closure. Similarly, a photochemical process will be *disrotatory* if k is even and *conrotatory* if k is odd.

Another example of an electrocyclic reaction is the ring opening of dimethyl *cis*-cyclobutene-1,2-dicarboxylate (I) on heating to yield dimethyl *trans,cis*-butadiene-1,4-dicarboxylate (II).

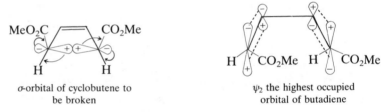

Conrotatory ring opening of cyclobutanedicarboxylate: $2k = 4$, i.e. k is even

Notice that the reaction is stereospecific and that the carboxylate groups have rotated in the same direction, i.e. *conrotatory*. If we look at the symmetry (this is the relative sign of the wave function) of the highest bonding orbitals, the *frontier orbitals*, involved in this reaction, we obtain the picture shown in Fig. 12.9. Notice that a bonding interaction is maintained between the orbitals concerned at all stages of the reaction.

σ-orbital of cyclobutene to
be broken

ψ_2 the highest occupied
orbital of butadiene

Fig. 12.9

Suprafacial and antarafacial interaction

When two olefinic or polyolefinic molecules interact (Fig. 12.10) they can do so on the same side of the molecular plane (a suprafacial interaction) or on opposite sides of the molecular plane (an antarafacial interaction).

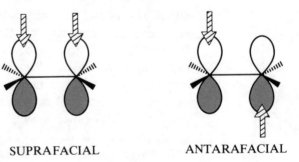

SUPRAFACIAL   ANTARAFACIAL

Fig. 12.10

An illustration of suprafacial and antarafacial interaction comes from the reaction of sulfur dioxide with 1,4-dimethylbutadiene and 1,6-dimethylhexatriene, called a *chele-tropic* reaction (Fig. 12.11).

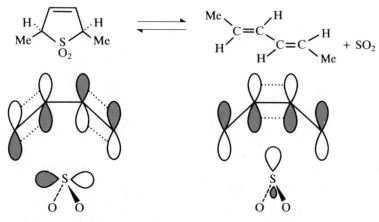

ψ_2 of butadiene interacting with vacant p-atomic orbital of the sulfur

ψ_3 of butadiene interacting with a filled hybrid atomic orbital of the sulfur

Fig. 12.11(*a*) Suprafacial interactions of sulfur dioxide with 1,4-dimethylbutadiene (*Disrotatory*)

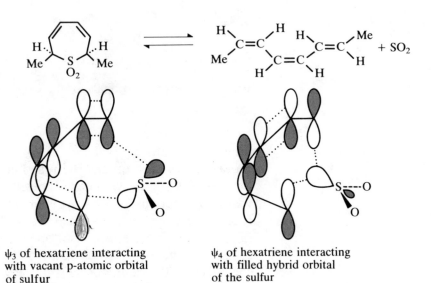

ψ_3 of hexatriene interacting with vacant p-atomic orbital of sulfur

ψ_4 of hexatriene interacting with filled hybrid orbital of the sulfur

Fig. 12.11(*b*) Antarafacial addition of sulfur dioxide to 1,6-dimethylhexatriene (*Conrotatory*)

Sigmatropic rearrangements

Sigmatropic is the name given by Woodward and Hoffman to molecular rearrangements involving the fission and formation of σ-bonds in a cyclic transition state. The two best examples are the Claisen rearrangement:

and the Cope rearrangement:

We can depict the relevant molecular orbitals in the Cope rearrangement as shown in Fig. 12.12. We have drawn the

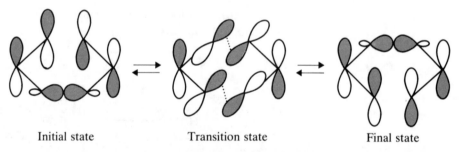

Initial state   Transition state   Final state

Fig. 12.12 Frontier orbitals for the Cope rearrangement: suprafacial–suprafacial

transition state as involving two allyl radicals, interacting suprafacial to each other. The reaction going from ground state to ground state is symmetry allowed. It is clearly possible to visualize reactions of this type involving longer chains if we regard the Cope rearrangement as a (3,3)-sigmatropic process, (3,3) signifying three centres of one reactant, reacting with three centres of the other, then (3,5) and (5,5) processes are also conceivable. The general rule is that if we define the order of the sigmatropic process as (i,j) where a σ-bond, flanked by one or more π-bonds, migrates to a new position, joined to atoms $i - 1$ and $j - 1$ removed from its original position, then if $i + j = 2k$, a thermal supra-supra process is symmetry allowed if k is odd, and a thermal supra-antara (or an antara-supra) process is symmetry allowed if k is even. Conversely a photochemical supra-antara (or an antara-supra) process is symmetry allowed if k is even and a supra-supra process if k is odd.

We have depicted the Cope rearrangement as involving a 'chair' shaped transition state with two allyl fragments interacting in a supra-supra fashion (i.e. $\pi_s^3 + \pi_s^3$). In fact the process is really $(\pi^2 + \sigma^2 + \pi^2)$. In order to define the stereochemistry precisely, we need to be able to classify the mode of the reaction at the σ-bond. We can do this as follows; if the reaction involves either a retention (r) at each end of the σ-bond or an inversion (i) at each end of the bond we designate the process suprafacial.

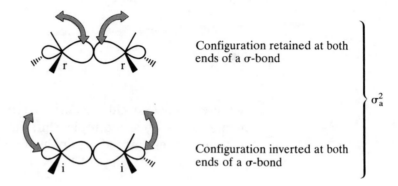

Configuration retained at both ends of a σ-bond

Configuration inverted at both ends of a σ-bond

σ_a^2

If the reaction involves an inversion at one end of a σ-bond and retention at the other, we designate the process antarafacial.

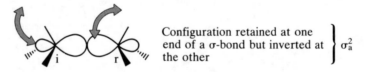

Configuration retained at one end of a σ-bond but inverted at the other

σ_a^2

Notice that the Cope rearrangement involving the type of interaction we depicted above now becomes $\pi_s^2 + \sigma_s^2 + \pi_s^2$ (Fig. 12.13).

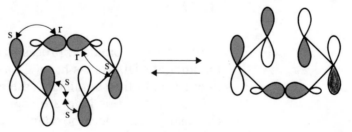

Fig. 12.13 $\pi_s^{2'} + \sigma_s^2 + \pi_s^2$. Symmetry allowed

We can now look back at the electrocyclic reactions. The symmetry allowed ring opening of cyclobutene is *conrotatory* and we can depict this as *either* suprafacial at the π-orbital and antarafacial at the σ-orbital *or* antarafacial at the π-orbital and suprafacial at the σ-bond (Fig. 12.14).

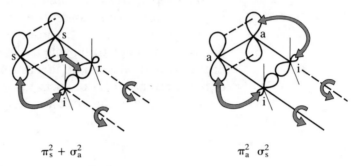

$$\pi_s^2 + \sigma_a^2 \qquad\qquad \pi_a^2\ \sigma_s^2$$

Fig. 12.14

We can now consider a further type of molecular rearrangement; the (i, j) sigmatropic shift in which a group or atom migrates within an all *cis*-polyene chain. An example is a 1,5-hydrogen shift (Fig. 12.15).

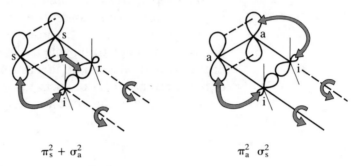

Suprafacial

Antarafacial

Fig. 12.15

Notice the suprafacial process has a plane of symmetry while the antarafacial process has a C_2 axis. We can depict the orbital interaction in the suprafacial case as in Fig. 12.16.

Reactions of this kind are common and important in organic chemistry. The decarboxylation of malonic and aceto-acetic ester derivatives have been much used in synthesis. These are

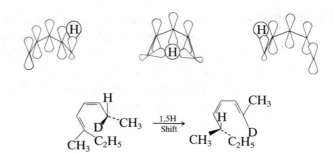

Fig. 12.16 1,5-Hydride shift in *cis*-penta-1-3-diene

typical examples of 1,5-hydride shifts:

β, γ-Unsaturated carboxylic acids

β-keto carboxylic acids

Malonic acids

(*a*) Decarboxylation reactions

Closely related are the formation of olefins from esters and vinyl ethers and the formation of ketene from acetic anhydride.

Vinyl ether

Ethyl acetate

$O:C:CH_2$

Acetic anhydride

(*b*) Loss of ethylene or ketene

All the reactions described in this chapter can be embraced in a simple law. If $2k$ is the total number of atoms involved in a supra-suprafacial cyclic process, then when k is odd, the reaction will proceed through the ground state. If k is even, a supra-suprafacial reaction will only proceed through excited states, but a supra-antarafacial process can occur through ground states.

Further reading

The Conservation of Orbital Symmetry, R. B. Woodward and R. Hoffmann, Academic Press, New York, 1970.
Organic Reactions and Orbital Symmetry, T. L. Gilchrist and R. C. Stove, Cambridge University Press, Cambridge, 1972.
Pericyclic Reactions, G. B. Gill and M. R. Wilkie, Chapman and Hall, London, 1974.
Pericyclic Reactions, Vols I and II, ed. A. P. Marchand and R. E. Lehr, Academic Press, New York, 1977.

Problems

1 Complete the following reaction sequences:

$$CH_3CH=CH-CH=CH_2 + MeOCOC\equiv CCOOMe \longrightarrow$$
$$CH_2=CH-CH=CH_2 + (NC)_2C=C(CN)_2 \longrightarrow$$
$$CH_2=\overset{\overset{\displaystyle CH_3}{|}}{C}-\underset{\underset{\displaystyle CH_3}{|}}{C}=CH_2 + (NC)_2C=O \longrightarrow$$
$$C_6H_5N_3 + MeOCOC\equiv CCO_2Me \longrightarrow$$

2 Use frontier orbital considerations to decide whether the following concerted reactions are effected thermally or photochemically.

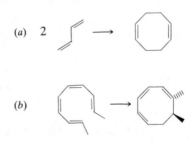

(c)

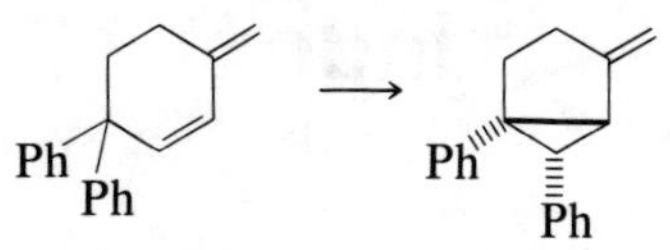

(d)

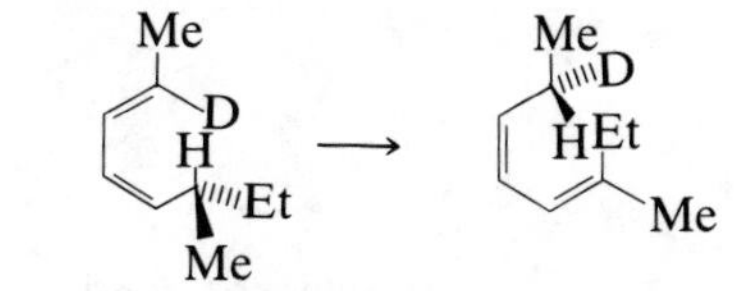

3 Account for the following reaction

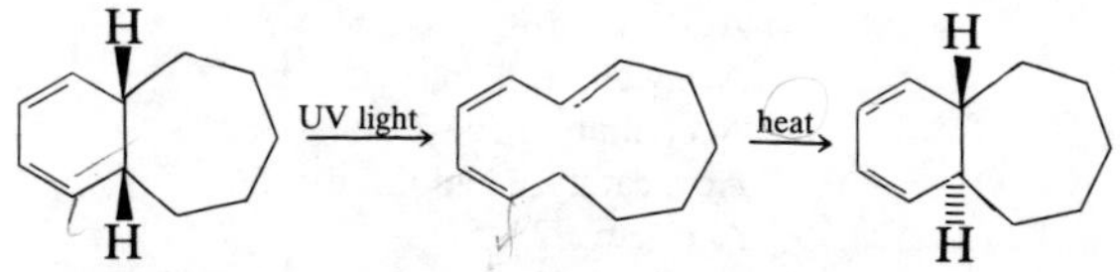

Index